Medicine
&
Duty

Medicine & Duty

A War Diary

By

Harold Dearden

(*Late Capt. R.A.M.C.*)

London
William Heinemann Limited

First Published
1928

Printed in Great Britain at The Windmill Press, Kingswood, Surrey

A WAR DIARY

INTRODUCTION

WHEN writing this diary nothing was
farther from my mind than that it should
ever be exposed to the public gaze. It came
into being, indeed, without any deliberate
plan on my part whatever. It was simply
that one's mind at the time was receiving
a ceaseless flood of new impressions of so
vivid and tumultous a character as impera-
tively to demand expression, and one
wrote to oneself, as it were, for no other
purpose than to make that expression
possible.

With so frankly egoistic an origin, an
insistence on my own thoughts and actions
was unavoidable ; but, as regards the latter
at least, I am comforted by the reflection
that they are of so undistinguished a
nature as to be inoffensive even to the most

rigid canons of reticence and modesty.
With this in view, however, I have elimi-
nated wherever possible all references of a
personal character with regard to my com-
panions. They would be the first to resent
praise ; and indeed in a company where
gallantry was a commonplace any com-
mendation of mine would be merely an
impertinence.

The material of the diary is necessarily
disjointed. It was written at odd times
and in odd places—in the mess, to the
accompaniment of a gramophone and
much conversation, or in dug-outs and aid-
posts to an accompaniment less pleasant
perhaps, but no less distracting in character. Much of it was sent home in the form
of letters to persons who, with a wisdom
which doubtless does them credit, destroyed or mislaid them, and as much of
it again was destroyed or mislaid as a
result of the chances inseparable from
one's environment. With these excep-
tions however, the thing remains as I

made it at the time. Not a word has been changed, and not a phrase turned ; and if at times there is more than a hint of a rawness that seems now deplorable, it serves, on a re-reading, merely to emphasize the effect on my mind of a narrative written by a stranger. Herein, indeed, lies its interest for me. It recalls much that would otherwise be as inaccessible as a previous incarnation; and if it should serve others of its readers in the same fashion I shall feel that it has, to that extent at least, justified its production. For of the earlier phases of the war I can remember nothing. I can see myself in August 1914 standing in the hall of the Bath Club, and staring with many others at a notice board covered with thrilling announcements of even the nature of which I am now entirely ignorant. Those were the days when to be " going out to France " was to be invested with glory and envied by one's friends. Men sought this privilege with the ardour of lovers, convinced that delay would see the end of hostilities and the frustration of their hopes. I was lucky. A Battalion was in process of being recruited to go overseas at once. I was appointed, by the kindness of a friend, to be Medical Officer to that Battalion, and my hopes were high, if unfounded.

I was escorted to my train, with Faulkner's dressing scarce dry upon my boots, by a friend ; and in the smoky gloom of Euston by midnight I pledged myself to do all that a friend might do to bring him in my wake. I may say that I succeeded in my efforts, and my friend was shortly gazetted to my side ; but it would be affectation to say that I recall, after the first few days, anything on his part which could in any way be construed into an expression of a sense of his obligation in the matter. For the Battalion, when recruited, did not go overseas. It remained indubitably a Battalion, but undeniably and distressingly static ; and the deepest gloom descended in consequence upon those who were its officers. The wildest rumours became current as to the fate of the Battalion—I recall being credibly informed on one occasion that it was to be equipped with bicycles, for some purpose not specified, but impossible at any rate to associate with the idea of " going to France "—and the wildest activities were indulged in therefore to get transferred to units whose future seemed brighter at the moment. From that time till I did reach France is merely a jumble of confused impressions. I served in hospitals whose surgical equipment was in inverse ratio to the number of their beds. I was at one time a Captain, at another a Major. I was even for a brief and halcyon period actually a Colonel—till subsequent investigations revealed the fact that I had no right whatever to that exalted station, and I descended with the same suggestion of enchantment that had seen my star arise. I recall, too, that my declension almost prostrated my housekeeper, to whom my gradations in martial brilliancy never ceased to be of importance. At length, however, I did reach France, by the simple method of going out under the aegis of the Red Cross, and getting myself metamorphosed—more enchantment—into the R.A.M.C. on the spot!

From there my diary commences; but no one is more conscious than I that as a history of the campaign of that period it is lamentably deficient in value. It is, to a history of the war, what a pantry-book is to the history of a great family. For of the war itself, of its subtle moves and momentous phases, I knew literally nothing. From the beginning to the end I was a mere camp-follower. I went hither and thither, doing my microscopic "bit" as best I might, but of the intelligent side of the conduct of war—if indeed there be any —I never even for one moment achieved the most fleeting of glimpses. I knew, I admit, with whom we were fighting;

and I responded quite normally to the highly efficient propaganda offered for my encouragement. But the reason of it all, or the purpose, were never for one moment clear to my intelligence. And there were times—long previous to the Post-War Revelation—when even the propaganda had to me the faintest hint of a prospectus.

I found myself, moreover, unreasonably clumsy at reconciling my present duties with my previous conception of the purpose of my calling. To succour the wounded, that they might with greater celerity return to wound or be wounded on a subsequent occasion, seemed subtly reminiscent of those dreadful ministrations offered to horses at a bull-fight. For there, too, in drab little places within earshot of the cheering, skilful hands patched and prodded agonized creatures back into the arena. And if in my case the patching was better, the prodding more subtle, and the creature itself even willing to return, these facts merely shifted the plane of the whole grim business from the illogical to the insane. With these intellectual deficiences to contend with, it seemed to me better to abandon the problem entirely ; and I mention them merely to explain to some extent the narrow orbit of my narrative.

One last word as to my title.

For all who went through the war those three words, " Medicine and Duty," are likely to retain for ever the simple beauty that once was theirs ; but to such as were denied that refining influence some explanation may be of interest.

When a soldier presented himself for treatment, especially in or near the trenches, his physician—by much training —was led to adopt towards him an attitude of mind guaranteed to ruin that same physician in the shortest possible time in any other place on earth. That is to say, he endeavoured to prove, exclusively to his own satisfaction, that there was nothing whatever the matter with his patient; and the fact that the latter rarely accepted his diagnosis did not in the least degree affect the nature of his treatment. Having arrived at this conclusion (and to the sufferer it must have seemed that nothing short of an audible death-rattle could prevent him from doing so) he was accustomed to administer a brisk aperient and mark his card " Medicine and Duty."

Those words seemed to me symbolic, for to the private soldier they epitomized the war. He took, during those four years, an astonishing amount of medicine, compounded of wet and cold, and agony and bloody sweat; and of the nobility with which he fulfilled his duty no one who saw it is likely to lose the memory. But of the many who saw it, not a few, alas ! lost that memory with their lives; and the others are mostly too busy ensuring their own survival to have much leisure for memories.

We are undeniably grateful to the Private Soldier, and in that capacity, indeed, little or nothing in the way of favour was denied him on his return. But the Private Soldier exists no longer; and with his disappearance has vanished also most of our sense of debt. Maybe the fault lay in the mere choice of nomenclature, and that all might have been different had he fought and bled for us, not as the Private Soldier, but simply under his true title as the Man in the Street. He would then be more easy to recognize, and there would be less talk now of Communism—and less cause, maybe, for its apprehension.

DEDICATION

On a certain evening in Flanders, a non-commissioned officer of one of the Regiments of Foot Guards received orders to find a fatigue party of eight men for duty next day. At dawn of that day the enemy attacked, and a shell carried away at the thigh both legs of that N.C.O. and left him in a dying condition on the muddy ground. He beckoned feebly to his officer to approach, with his last remaining strength raised himself on his elbow, and whispered, " You'll not forget, sir, we have to find that fatigue party to-day." So saying, he died.

To the memory of that gallant fellow, and of that same spirit animating his regiment with which for a time I had the privilege of serving, I would dedicate this simple story of what was, in all sincerity, one of the happiest periods of my life.

those rooms where juries wait in dismal apprehension before going to view the body.

We have three small lamps in the room, which is about as large as a ten-acre field; and we have fifteen men in the mess. The result is that all three lamps are huddled round the central stove for warmth, and round these four faintly glowing points are clustered all fifteen of the mess.

Since most men out here read merely between intervals of talking or playing the piano, and since most of the furniture in the room seems to have been designed primarily with a view to table-turning, the inducement to connected thought is really not very striking. However, they are a very good crowd, and very cheery, and time flies quickly and agreeably. But one's best recipe for happiness out here consists in a reversion to one's early Varsity days, when men did not probe too deeply into anything, and any leanings towards spirituality or sentiment were taken as indications

2

of some secret moral aberration, and therefore encouraged accordingly. On the whole it is quieter in one's bedroom than anywhere; but writing with the block on the window-sill is of a coldness outside my previous experience, so I brave the mess instead. I was delighted to-day at lunch to hear a man telling another what a lot of good this war had done to his brother. " He was a namby pamby sort of chap before, used to read a lot and that sort of thing, you know ; no real harm in him but a useless sort of beggar. Now he's had three years as a private in the 3rd London, and he's as decent a fellow as you could want to know!" It is good to know that the war is uplifting people after all, as the Bishop of London so encouragingly said.

We get some cases through here, too. I am orderly officer to-day, and am writing this in the O.O.'s sitting room—a cheerful place, furnished simply but tastefully with a deal table, a stove, and two chairs, one of

3

which shows marked signs of having been " used and thrown away," as the novelists say. There is also a bed with " fittings," the latter being very attractively displayed by the orderly inside an empty drug case, the open side of which is turned towards the world in general. When I say that I go elsewhere to wash, you can form a pretty accurate picture of the " fittings."

An orderly has just been in to tell me that we must expect two trains to-night, " any time after ten," one with 40 lying and 60 sitting, and the other with 60 lying and 30 sitters, so there will be little or no sleep for the unfortunate O.O. to-night.

I was orderly officer last night, which entails receiving all convoys of wounded, and, incidentally, getting about one hour's sleep ; but it's full of interest and human nature. Once when I was standing on the top of the steps about 2.30 a.m., waiting to receive a convoy, a 'bus full of walking cases unloaded at the gates. As they came along the road up to the door they made a wonderful picture—such typical fighting men, mud-stained and practical, with their steel helmets swung behind them, and their bandaged hands and heads and mud-splashed faces and hair. But as the first man came into the full glare of the arcs over the door, it was as though something magical had happened. It took my breath away. Quite gone was the grim khaki figure of a second before, and there, under the faded fancy dress, was just a dog-tired little cockney, thin neck, adenoids and all. As he saw me standing in the shadow he gave his pack a pathetic little hitch, pulled himself up, and saluted with his one good hand—but it was the real heart of the man that I had seen for that one second when he thought he was alone. It made quite an impression on me, and I could not help thinking what a story it would make

5

if one could translate to paper that boy's thoughts, as he dragged himself—cold and leg-weary—up those few steps nearer Blighty !

There is one incident, too, which always pleases me when the Sergeant is filling in their ward cards, his questions being asked in order of their occurrence on the card, and entirely without reference to any sequence of thought. They are put in a very loud and toneless voice, with just that suggestion that you are alive to any attempt on his part to deceive you which is official when dealing with the private soldier, and the following takes place regularly:—

"Name ?   Jones, A. L.
"Number ?   2734
"Religion ?   C. of E.

Then, quickly, to catch him off his guard —" Have you got a jack knife with you ? " I have heard it put like that to a semitone some thousands of times now, and yet it's ever fresh to me, even at four in the morn-

6

ing when my feet are occupying a semi-detached existence from the rest of my sensibilities—the association of ideas and questions is so perfectly grotesque ; and yet no flicker of the humour of it has ever penetrated to the Sergeant's efficiency.

I never go to bed here without a look of amazement over my untroubled mind. One shares it with successful nuns and ploughmen of the healthier sort, I suppose; and it springs doubtless from a robust system, and an absence of all things savouring of introspection. At any rate it is something I have not experienced myself for many years; and, like a happy husband, I turn sometimes and lie awake to wonder at my bed-fellow !

Had a very interesting day. A heavy convoy in last night, with a good many badly-wounded and gassed. Saw one man,

7

an Irishman about 60 years old, who had bad rheumatic pains and a very irregular heart—obviously unfit to be out here. When I had gone over him pretty thoroughly I signed him up H.S.C.* for England, and told him so.

"You're for England to-day, boy," I said, and expected to see him smile the beam they all give when you tell them so. Instead he looked absolutely distressed and said nothing.

"Don't you want to go home?" I asked. He looked very uncomfortable, almost as if he were going to cry, and——

"I volunteered to come out here," he said; "I'm really very strong, it's only these aches that get a bit bad at times."

It fairly took my breath away, the spirit and keeness of the old man were so above words. I finally cheered him up by saying we had to send plenty of men half his age home for a few weeks when they had been out here a good while, and that at the end

*Hospital Ship case

8

of his rest he would be as fit as ever and able to come out and do his job again. But they're wonderful people.

Sister called me at 3.30 this morning to see a man who came in yesterday with a bullet in the spine, and who was very bad, she said. Went down and found him vomiting blood, temp. 103, pulse very rapid and too feeble to count—obviously running out. I talked to him for a bit. He was quite clear and said he felt a good deal better than he did when he came in, which is curious but very common before death. About an hour later, while I was holding him sideways to vomit, he just flopped through my hands with the blood still running down his face and died then and there. He was a good fellow ; 37, and a shopkeeper in Darlington. I went afterwards to give an intravenous injection of ether for an anæsthetic. The man was a French Canadian, both legs badly shattered by shell fire, and needed double amputation. They were very short of orderlies, so I lent a hand to lift him from his bed on to the stretcher. He was in great pain in any position and movement only aggravated it. He was also terribly nervous and had completely lost all self-control. He didn't want to be moved at all and kept on calling out, " I can't bear any more, you'll only hurt me;" and then when we did lift him he rose into a scream of " I knew you would, I knew you would ! Oh ! Oh !" and kept it up all the way into the theatre and until he was under the anæthetic. He was a small-ish man to begin with ; and when he had his two legs off at the thigh he looked like a tortured child somehow—so little, almost inhuman.

I saw a wonderful letter to-night when censoring, from a Canadian battery driver to another man in the same battery up the line. The writer has both legs badly shattered but is doing well, and goes to England to-morrow.

This is his letter.

" Dear Bill,

" I am taking the pleasure in writing a few lines hopeing this finds you in good health well old boy I'm going to Blighty tomorrow so I gues you have lost me for good now. I'm afraid I shall not be back again for a long time now but I will write and tell you how I get on, remember me to all the boys, tell Mack and Wood and Dick I'll write to them to, when I was in the train I saw one of my chums from the 37th Battery Winnipeg, poor chap he had his head cut about something fierce I did feel that sorry for him. Well Bill, try your hardest to get my team of horses has you know they can't be beat, it's a lovely team and if you get them look after them old boy has you know I did, and they knew it, and don't hit Nell that's the mare, if you do she won't pull that's why I never trouble about a whip now. so long Bill

                    " Yours truly

" P.S.—Please send my things down

after me, you can have my sox and
tobacco, good luck."

You'd travel a long way and read a good
many better written letters without meet-
ing a cleaner, kinder, or straighter soul
than this half-educated fellow's.

It's raining like the devil and a high
wind getting up, so I'll just go down and
see if there's any news of a convoy, and if
not, I'll push off to bed. I had scarcely
written " bed " when an orderly came in
to say, " eight officers and fourteen other
ranks just arrived, sir." So I shall not go
to bed just yet, after all ! Time—12.15
a.m.

A little fox terrier has just come creeping into the hospital and taken refuge on
the bed of one of the patients who is sleeping out in the garden. She is a wretched
little cowed thing, and seems half wild with
terror, is a mass of dirt, and looks as if

she had been chased for miles and stoned.
The man is quite pleased to have her on
his bed, and I have told an orderly to get
her a plate of food.

Was called at four this morning by Night
Sister to come and look at a Tetanus man
who was very bad, she said. Found him
with quite definite spasms, his jaw tight
shut and looking like a horrible wooden
image with that same fixed grin they all
get. He was in terrible pain with the
spasms; and between them kept asking
" How long will this last for, Doctor ? "
Of course, he was hopeless ; so I said, " Oh
not long now, boy ; this first stage is always
the worst; when you get over this, you'll
be as right as rain ;" and sent Sister down
for the chloroform. I kept him under until
nine o'clock, when he died.

A very quiet day. Got up feeling very
seedy and cheap, and fear I must have a

touch of " flue " or something. Fortunately
no convoy has come in, and as we have
an almost empty hospital after last night's
evacuation there's little or nothing to do.
A very strong rumour prevails that all
correspondence between England and here
is going to be stopped without warning.
The spy system is so difficult to control,
and the big push coming on makes it impossible to take risks. I hope it proves as
false as most of our rumours.

The little dog is still great friends with
the man she chose first, and lies on his bed
all day and night. He has tied a bow of
cyanide gauze round her neck, and con-
fided to me to-day that he has called her
" Alice," after a dog that he has at home,
and that even already she understands
everything he says. As she is a French
dog I should doubt it ; but she certainly
loves him all right, and lies up against the
cradle over his broken leg as happy as
can be.

If no convoy comes to-night I shall have

a hot bath and clear off to bed early ; I feel like a boiled owl at present.

Another quiet day.

The Hospital is nearly empty, no new cases came in last night, and we have scarcely anything to do in the surgical line.

Went up to the tennis court in the afternoon and watched the tennis ; talked for about three hours to the girls there—to improve my French !—and was fetched back at six o'clock by an orderly to see a case who was bleeding. Came back to find a lad who has a badly shattered knee bleeding pretty badly, and tied two small vessels. He is only about twenty and a very decent lad. It seems awful to think sometimes of the number of armless and legless men we have turned out of this hospital alone. England will be a quaint place after this is all over.

Got up feeling very seedy and rotten this morning—a fearful head and a filthy tongue. Sat indoors all the afternoon ; very few cases in the hospital, so there was little or nothing to do. About five o'clock I strolled up to the tennis courts for an hour or two. Great amusement caused by a V.A.D.'s knickers making a really sporting attempt to come down in the middle of a fierce rally.

Came home and had a hot bath ; couldn't look at dinner ; so cleared off to bed after a small convoy of eight officers and four men had arrived at about 10.30.

Was up all night with dysentery, and got out of bed this morning feeling like nothing on earth. Had quite made up my mind to go back to bed after my morning round, but the other men told me I looked so done up when I came in for breakfast that they insisted on my going straight back to bed then and there. I wasn't sorry to go, as a matter of fact, so here I am.

To-day being Corpus Christi day there was a procession of the Catholics through the town, and a very quaint sight it was. I only saw a very little of it, which was annoying, for it was very picturesque, with rows of little children got up as angels, and the ground all strewn with artificial or real green grass. All sorts of incongruous mixtures of people walked, some in full evening dress with silk hats in their hands, and several very gelatinous-looking priests, holding their books very near their noses, and singing most damnably out of tune. Just before the main body came along I had to obey an urgent summons and flee away, and before I could get back it was all over. Very annoying, for it was a curious affair.

Felt much better this morning, but they will not let me up till my blood report comes. It has rained practically all day. About twelve o'clock the gun went off, which signals the approach of a Taube, and a few seconds later the anti-aircraft guns opened fire. I looked out of the window but could see nothing, and in a minute or so it was quiet again.

Sister brought the little dog up to see me, and she stayed all day on my bed. It was quite nice having her ; and I told her a few things about my Tim, which doubtless astonished her !

Have been reading all day Guy de Maupassant, Mrs. Balfame and a book, *Les Civilizés*, lent me by Sister. The last named consists mainly in fairly vivid descriptions of opium-smoking and other esoteric hobbies. Sister said it was "lurid, but beautifully written ; " so perhaps I may get the charm of style soon !

Up to-day at last, and very glad, too. Feel pretty groggy about the knees and back, but very fit otherwise.

We have only twelve men and four officers in the entire hospital, so if a rush comes we shall have a pretty gay time before us.

A car has stopped outside the hospital to call for the Colonel; and it has an exhaust with exactly the note and metre of my old Rolls at home. It makes me feel quite homesick to hear it out there, with everything so still and heavy in the evening air. Censoring the letters to-night I came across two which I have copied out. As human documents they are really unique. The first is from the father of a fellow who is dying fast of sepsis, with a compound fracture of both thighs. His father, who is a farmer in Ireland, was wired for by the War Office that his son was on the " dangerous " list, and came over to see him. He arrived to-day; and this is his letter home to his wife. The boy is the only one they have ; he is still quite conscious, and thinks he is going to get all right again in time. He's a nice lad, with great bony shoulders, enormous white blue-veined hands on the end of grotesquely thin arms, and a beard which defies the daily efforts of the barber to keep his chin smooth.

This is the old man to his wife, literally:

" Dear Sara—I have arrived with Joe and am sorry to say the Doctors say he will be dead very soon now. I landed about three o'clock, he sends his very best love, and says he hopes to see you soon, dear Sarah; it makes my heart sore to see how he has shrunk away from so fine a boy to this. It was a long journey, but I do not mind; he was very pleased to see his dad, he says. Dear Sara, you must not take on too much, they have been real good to him hear. I shall try and make up to you for this trouble, Sara, this is a fine place. I wish I could have brought Joe home with me, it will

20

be a long journey back going alone.
Your loving husband."

I saw him when he arrived at the hospital, sitting very upright in the Y.M.C.A.
car which brought him from the boat, and
afterwards standing very shyly in the hall
—black coat, umbrella, and neat bowler
hat—looking curiously small and pathetic
among so much movement and efficiency.
One feels it will indeed be a long journey
home.

The second letter is from a Canadian
private, shot through both lungs, but doing
fairly well. He is long, incredibly long—
he seems almost to overflow from the head
and foot of his bed—and he has the most
fascinating drawl you can imagine. He
has a terrific shock of straw-coloured hair
also, that hangs down over his bony forehead, and the clearest blue eyes over a big,
loose-lipped, humorous mouth. He chews
gum, very deliberately, all day ; and at
meal times he disposes of his gum temporarily by attaching it to his bed rail, in the

same natural way that I might put down a cigar. He said he found the ward stuffy, so I had his bed moved outside, where, as he says, "It's good to see a bit of stuff growing." He is quietly sure he is going to get better, as witness his letter to his brother in Ontario.

"Dear Bob—I'm in hospital here, and am feeling about the same. My old chest feels as if there was a half dozen iron bands round it. I sleep outside now, and do it fine, I couldn't manage the ward at all. This is a dandy hospital, they sure treat you white, if I didn't want to see Blighty so much I'd stay here till my old chest is fixed up and glad. Well, how is things in the old berg ? I wish the war was over and I was home again. There hasn't been no warm weather over here since I come. How is Bella ? I suppose she has boxed you ears good and plenty since you been married. Is mother still feeling good, to bad if her legs get sore again. Well, old man, this is all I can manage now, God bless you and tell Mother I said so to her to, From your bro: Tom."

To-day I took a stroll up the hill towards the lighthouse. It was a glorious evening, wonderfully still and clean-smelling after the rain, and the frogs were making an astonishing noise in the ditch along the roadside. As I came back towards the town, I met some girls from the village walking with some boys who had just been " called up." The boys had flowers in their coats, and coloured paper streamers tied to their caps, as they all do when they get their " papers." They were laughing and swaggering a good deal, and gave me a very glorified salute as we passed, which amused the girls immensely. We were just in the dip of the valley under the little village church. There is a great wooden crucifix looking quietly down over the village ; and just over a little red-tiled wall was a " K "-legged old man working with a long-handled spade—taking in an-

23

other field for the Cemetery, in time for the summer and the "big push." I thought, if some of those lads had noticed him, they might have put their streamers in their pockets and started asking themselves questions.

Had a very thrilling day to-day. Heard from —— to say he was going over from Poperinge to Dunkirk for the afternoon and asking me to meet him. As we had cleaned out every case but the serious ones, and I was feeling a bit tired, I got a pass after much difficulty and motored over to Dunkirk.

A lovely sunny day, and the car running well. Went *via* Calais, and a very interesting trip it was. All the fields were full of women, scarcely any men except very old ones and cripples. And the mustard was in full bloom. The women

looked very picturesque in their big head-
dresses, pushing the quaintest little hand-
hoes like perambulators ; and there were
quite wee children carrying enormous
loads of weeds. It's a curious sight, too, to
come upon a long row of women weeding in
a field, with their backs all turned towards
you. They bend down from the hips,
with a straight knee, quite unlike a man ;
and the effect is a row of very dull skirts,
down in front and up behind, enough to
show a pair of coarse stockings up to the
knees, and then—bang ! like a Daly's
Chorus—up come all the bright white
heads as they stand to look round at the
car ! Quite a pretty sight. Saw a lovely
girl, too, standing outside a cottage by a
forge. She made quite a picture as she
looked sideways towards us, with her short
skirt and splendid bust, and her left hand
raised in such a pretty gesture to hold her
wind-blown hair out of her eyes.

The women here of that class are often
very pretty ; but the men are a dreary lot,

all moustaches, and long cigarette holders, with yellow boots just showing under their puttees—which latter they contrive to wind almost as far as their toes. A dirty, unkempt lot; it's quite a treat to see our smart fellows with their well-fitting khaki, flat backs, and cheery faces, with a jaunty woodbine behind their ear, and a "don't-care-a-damn-for-anything" air about them which suits them down to the ground.

I saw five Tommies in Dunkirk kiss a girl and pass her along all five of them ; and they did it with such a cheery, damned breath-snatching air of impertinence that not even a Duchess could have objected. Certainly the girl didn't ; for she ran laughing into a shop and banged the door in the face of the sixth lad, a slow, short, twisted-looking little elderly man, who was carrying a big brown paper parcel which dripped cherries as he ran. I can imagine him always late for everything, and the cheery, hardy butt of the Canteen.

Calais is a dreary hole, rather like Blackpool with the sea taken away, and we didn't stay in it any longer than was necessary. Dunkirk, too, is rather a dismal place, but it has the interest that all places possess which have been under fire.

The windows in the square where the church is are all boarded up above the first floor, and the church is simply a large heap of ruins.

It is quaint, too, to see, as you walk along a street, a notice posted up over certain sheltered passages between houses, *Refuge en cas d'alerte,* and to have your eye constantly caught by the white splashes of shrapnel-marks on the dirty grey stone of the houses.

The town is full of Belgian troops, and it's impossible to tell officers from men except by the fact that the former spit rather less dexterously and have longer cigarette holders. No one salutes anyone else, and on the whole one's pity for King Albert increases every time you pass one of his gallant troops. —— and his two fellow M.O.'s dragged me round to a noted tea-shop, where there is reputed to be a " bit of stuff " ; and I'm bound to say we were not disappointed. There are really two " bits " normally, but one was engaged with a party of officers in a front room, so we were ministered to by the other portion. She was fairly good-looking in a coarse way, dark, big-chested and greasy about the nose and forehead as they all are, with her back hair apparently growing right away down out of sight on her neck ; and a series of little dirty pin-heads running symmetrically back along the parting in her hair. I longed to order her a shampoo lotion ! Her two modes of entertaining were, firstly, to show you the pictures in a very clever work called *La Nue de la Theatre*—real photos of ninth-rate music-hall artistes with nothing on doing tedious things with very dirty-looking men who, to do them justice, looked thoroughly bored with the whole affair.

Having broken the ice, as it were, by this

means, she proceeded by endeavouring to put her hands in our trouser pockets—a ruse combining the advantages of enabling her at once to give pleasure to us and also to pick up any loose cash that might be there. After a while, one of the men, who had been eight months up the line and could scarcely be called hypercritical, said, " I say, this is a monstrous woman ; whose idea was this boring place ? " Whereupon, no one dissenting, we went out and had tea in the hotel like human beings.

Having shown ourselves capable of really subtle humour by exchanging the plates bearing the words " Dames " and " Hommes," which occupied a prominent position on the deserted first floor of the hotel, we went out again and got into our respective cars to come home.

They were very keen for me to put up for a Casualty Clearing Station job and ask to be appointed to theirs, but a Battalion job is what I really want. Had a very amusing day, but I should say humour

of the "Hommes" and "Dames" type
would pall on me after a while !

Did not go to bed till very late last night,
or, rather, early this morning. Going round
the wards this morning I saw them dressing the Endocarditis lad, and lent a hand
with one or two things. As he was being
propped up in bed afterwards, I saw they
had got the pillows all wrong, with his
back in a hollow and his head shoved forward on his neck ; so I went afterwards
and re-arranged them all for him, and
when it was done I asked him "How's
that ?" He wriggled his head back into
them and said, "That's just fine !" and
smiled all over his wide mouth at me. In
the evening, when Sister was doing his
pillows again for him, he told her, "You
can't do that like the Boss," so as I was in
the ward she came and told me, and I went
and did them again for him. "That's the

ticket ! " he said, and smiled triumphantly
up at Sister, as though he'd scored off her
beautifully ; and to my amazement she
had her eyes full of tears. I couldn't help
thinking, when I was holding him up and
doing his pillows, of the hundreds of times
at home I used to do poor ——'s before she
died, and how she would never let anyone
else touch them, and used to send the nurse
up to me at night to come down and do
them. How far away all that seems now.

Saw one lad's knee, which we have been
hanging on to, hoping it would quieten
down ; but now his general condition is
such that he would never stand the strain.
We arranged to do it in the afternoon and
amputated it just above the knee. The
lad was very good when I told him I
thought he'd better have it off, but he
looked straight ahead of him and said
nothing—just looked, with his poor thin
nostrils working like a rabbit's, and shoot-
ing a dry dirty tongue out every few
seconds to moisten his gluey lips. I don't

31

think he heard many of the lies I told him about men who could do everything with an artificial leg that they could ever do before, but there is really nothing else you can say. Went for a walk in the afternoon, and could hear the guns sounding as though they were twenty yards off. What it must be like to be really near them, God knows.

Had a good specimen of a gas helmet given me by a patient to-day, it will make a very interesting souvenir.

When I went up to dinner, there was such a gale blowing that you couldn't stand on the balcony. I'm afraid it's going to make things harder for the push, for you can't use gas in a gale like this, and bringing up guns is infinitely more difficult, too.

Another very busy day. A good many cases came in this morning, several pretty bad. Amputated one boy's leg; he's only just eighteen, and looks so bad that I doubt if he will live the night through. His mother and sister are here with him ; but he hasn't properly recovered from the anæsthetic yet, so I don't think he will know them again before he goes.

In the afternoon, as I had had no fresh air for two days, I took the car to the town and had tea in *the* tea-shop. It was crowded with officers, and inferior French harlots sitting round with their legs crossed, showing all their calf and about two inches of their thigh. One girl opposite me had a white frock and stockings on ; and her legs—long, very thin and sharp about the shin, and almost as thin and flat in the thigh—were the most pitiful things I've seen for a long while. She saw me looking at them intently, and I imagine thought I was a conquest, for she came and sat at the next table and smiled. I gave her my copy of the *Autocar*, which I'd just bought, and came away.

Got back to find a number more stretchers in, and several " sitters," and we are rapidly filling up. One man was lying in bed having his tea, with a compound fracture of the thigh. He was a miner from Newcastle, and told me he'd been over the German side of his parapet for eleven hours before he could be got in. They were using machine guns all the time and he thought every second he'd get another somewhere ; but here he is now putting away a round of bread and butter as happy as can be, and his nerves, at any rate, seem none the worse. One man tells me we have pushed them back 1000 metres over a front of 40 miles ; I hope it's true. He says they are no use at close quarters ; as he says, " they screamed like —— when we jumped into the trench." Another convoy of eight has just arrived, or rather seven ; one was dead when he was lifted out of the ambulance. I've just had a look at the amputation case, too, and he's obviously going fast. He's quite conscious now, and feeling no pain ; and he just holds your hand and rocks his head from

34

side to side, and keeps saying, " I'm all right now, sir ; just give me something to do, anything you like, sir, I'm all right now, sir," and so on and on without a pause. You can't count his pulse, his face is the colour of cream on a glass of milk, and the red oozing stump of his leg sticks straight up into the air like some horrible thing in Chinese lacquer. I've had to send his sister out, for she's crying so that she disturbs the other men ; but his mother is there still, trying to give him water out of a feeding cup. Every time he swings his head the spout strikes on his projecting teeth and she pours a jet down his chin and neck. He knows nothing about it, however, and it gives her something to do; so I've told her to give him one sip only at a time, but as often as she likes. I'm afraid he'll stop before she tires, poor soul.

It's just after one o'clock, so I'll push off to bed.

Very busy day. Had a good many opera-
tions in the morning and one or two in the
afternoon. The amputation boy died last
night about 3.30, and two of the three we
operated on after lunch don't look like
doing anything either.

Two heavy convoys came in this evening, and I am just writing this in the
interval while the theatre staff and all of
us are having cocoa and biscuits. Time,
1.15. Sergeant has just brought a message
to say we may expect eight stretchers any
time after two o'clock, so that will just
give us time to finish this next job and by
that time they will be here.

Did not go to bed last night till about
3 a.m. A very heavy convoy came in early
this morning, and we have been busy all
morning clearing them out to England,
and elsewhere. They are a very bad lot of
injuries, and I suppose will continue to be
so as long as we are attacking.

36

The news everywhere is very good. Colonel has just been in and told me we are making good headway all along the line, and the men all talk with the utmost confidence—though they have never done anything else, it's true. My Endocarditis lad went to England this morning to die. I was passing through the hall, and Sergeant told me he had been asking for me all morning since he heard he was to go at eight, and wanted to say good-bye. When they told him I hadn't got to bed till late, and was having my breakfast, he wouldn't let them disturb me; but when he saw me in the hall he shouted out from the ambulance, which was being filled in outside the door, and was quite glad to see me to say " good-bye." The abdominal man is dying fast, and we have three others and one officer who don't look very good, so I suppose we must expect a bad time.

It's a glorious day, with a light south-west wind, so we shall be able to use our gas on these unfortunate Allemands to some effect, which all helps, I suppose. A worthy thought—and a fitting response to the gift of God which has prompted it. In pre-war days so perfect a thing would have aroused in me none but the most banal and sloppy aspirations. Clearly then I am not so base as to be quite immune from " uplift." Am dining out to-night, but I imagine I shall be called away early. I hear I must expect very heavy convoys later to-day.

Two more ambulances full just arrived.

We have a curious case in just now. A soldier was told off to chop a tree down; and while doing so he missed the tree and his axe hit the ground, exploding a Mill's bomb buried there, and blowing the front of his abdominal wall away. He's pretty sure to die ; but it gives one a faint idea of the condition of affairs which will prevail after the war, with thousands of dud shells and bombs lying around.

I was called away to a convoy about 9.30 last night, and was hard at it until about 2 a.m., as more and more kept coming in. Sometimes the hall was so full of stretchers that it was hard to tell who were coming in and who were waiting to be taken down to the boat. Some of the wounds are perfectly appalling. I have never conceived anything could be so smashed up and yet live.

There is one man of about 33 with the entire front wall of his abdomen blown away, so that dressing him is a matter largely of keeping his intestines out of the bed. He is dying fast. He just lies and vomits with that easy grace that all peritonitis cases get; and his face with his pain, the shock, and the morphia he has had is just a writhing, twisting sheet of sweating grey linen. He never speaks, just lies there and dies. I'm writing this on a chair in the garden before lunch, and from where I am I can hear another man groaning. He has half his buttocks blown clean away; and though he has had morphia he just groans and groans till he has got almost a habit of it, and will stop if you sit and talk to him, but recommences immediately you leave him.

One of our sisters here is a curious creature, about 35, with an amazing figure; a very common Lancashire girl, as " fast " as it is possible to imagine anyone to be. She has beautiful black hair which is always very carefully dressed, and her clothes invariably look the height of care and neatness. She is, in addition, an absolutely first-class surgical nurse and has her heart in her work; and she is a born " helper," as the following little incident showed.

I went into her ward last night to see if all cases were being cleared out that were possible, and as a new convoy had just come in the place was like a beehive. Always before, when I have gone in, she has been full of indescribable wiles and lures, all softness and low-voiced questions

—in fact, all in the window. Last night, on the other hand, she just bustled about and did her job, with her apron all wet and sloppy, her face a bit smeared with dust, and a big piece of hair sticking to her sweating forehead. She took no notice at all of me as a man, but just took her orders and went round lifting and dressing as hard as ever she could, so gently and thoughtfully—obviously the best side of her all out. I was signing some cards at the table when she came up to cut some tubing for a drain for a man's leg. I looked up at her, and she said quite naturally and sincerely, " I wish you'd not come in if you can help it; I know I'm looking perfectly hideous, and it makes me wretched to have you see me like this." I said, " Quite honestly, Sister, I've never seen you looking so attractive "—but it was quaint how her old nature just popped out for a second like that.

Saw two perfectly wonderful letters in the mail last night, one from a lad to his

mother describing the taking of a trench—
" When we jumped into their trench,
mother, they all held up their hands and
shouted ' Camerad, Camerad,' and that
means ' I give in ' in their langwidge. But
they ad to have it, mother. I think that
is all from your loving Albert." " They
ad to have it," just delights me.

The other was from a married man to
his wife, who had evidently been warning
him against the temptations out here, and
urging him to be true to her. He said,
" You needn't think I shall get fond of any
of these French girls out here, I don't
think any of them can hold a candle to
my little woman. I've not been with but
two since I came out here so you see it's
all right." One imagines that three times
would have almost constituted infidelity !

Got to bed about one o'clock and was
called at 3.15 to another convoy of 26,

and have been at it ever since till now—
6.15 a.m.

Went for a walk along the shore to-day,
and saw some French lads and men playing with a seagull. The poor beast had
one wing broken, and they had managed
to catch it and tie a cord round its neck.
The sport consisted in poking it with a
stick till it made a desperate effort to fly
away, and then bringing it up with such a
tug of the cord that it lay open-beaked and
helpless on its back, till the next series of
pokes should rouse it to another effort.

For the sum of five francs I became the
possessor of a draggled heap of feathers
out of which blazed still a pair of indomit-
able eyes, and a beak which, when I tucked
him in the crook of my elbow, had just
enough strength left to seize my finger
with pitiful feebleness and hang on to it
till we reached home—game to the last !
I've put him in a box in my bedroom,
where with the aid of a penholder I feed
him with scraps of meat and fish which he

43

otherwise persistently refuses. When he's well enough I'll turn him out in the garden.

Had another busy day to-day, very heavy convoys in several times, and three heavy evacuations. I hear that we have had sixty thousand casualties so far in this push, but that Joffre, Haig and Co. are extremely pleased with the way things are going. I hear that when a large party of German prisoners, about 150, were being escorted back, they suddenly turned on their escort, took their rifles off them, and shot them down. A party of Australians who saw it from a distance came up at a double and shot every one. A wounded officer in here also says that he and a small escort were bringing about eighty prisoners back when one of them pulled a bomb out of his pocket and threw it at the officer, killing one man and wounding two others, including the officer.

44

This evening after tea I went for an hour or two into the town for some fresh air. Coming home I was just in time to see the mail boat in ; and there were dense masses of troops which had just arrived forming up on the quay side and in the market square across the bridge. It was fine to see them looking so fit and well and keen. I always think ours is a dismal sort of job, cooped up in hospitals, compared to theirs. I have just been round getting everything ready, and laying down stretchers in the coach house and under the awning in the garden, and everywhere where we can possibly find room. It's astonishing how much there is to do and think about. There has been the most glorious sunset to-night that I have ever seen, a perfectly wonderful array of colours, with one jet black cloud like a fairy boat in a perfect clear green sea of sky.

45

Have got another septic finger to-day which I have had opened up under gas this morning. They are more of a nuisance than anything else, for, by the time you have had the fomentation and dressing on you might as well have your hand in a feather-bed.

Had another busy day; was operating all afternoon from 1.45 till six o'clock without a break. At six o'clock I got a lift on a lorry with Sister —— to a little village on the sea-shore near here. It was a lovely evening with a perfect sunset, and we sat on the shore and talked for about an hour. Came home to find twenty-seven new cases just arriving, and was up in the theatre till 12.15.

I seem to get no time to do my diary these days. I'm generally so drowsy after I've finished work that I'm too stupid to write. Then the *Daily Mail* comes in in the evenings; and I generally take that to bed, read it, and fall asleep over the photos of disconslate Huns on the back page—quite forgetting the dismal Englishmen whom I have spent all day probing for iron.

Had a very interesting case to-day. A man had his arm very badly shattered a few days ago, and had practically the whole of the upper part blown away, leaving a wound from about his shoulder to half an inch from his elbow—a great gaping channel oozing pus. As suppuration increased his vessels began to rot and bleed, and finally he had one very heavy hemorrhage which nearly killed him. Fortunately I happened to be in the ward just when it came on; and as soon as sister took his dressings off a great jet of blood shot out across the floor and I had to catch hold of the artery in the wound with my fingers and hang on while they sent for another M.O. who anæsthetized him on the bed, and so we tied the vessel properly.

47

This loss of blood, however, left him absolutely pulseless and blanched, and it was obvious that he could never fight against his sepsis in that state. So we got a fellow who was slightly wounded and would otherwise go to the trenches again next day to consent to be bled, on condition of being sent to Blighty as a reward; and we transfused him. The result was literally magical. The man—who had been before but a bleached, pulseless, whining coward, who screamed and shed tears at the sight of a hypodermic needle and had never smiled for days—became a new man before our very eyes. His colour came back, he began to take an interest in what was going on, and became a really cheery, plucky fellow of the best type—and all within seven or ten minutes ! I have never seen anything which impressed me more. The man became a new man. His mental outlook as well as his physical appearance improved with every teaspoonful of healthy blood the other fellow pumped into him, and he went back to bed rosy and cheery. He has continued to improve and should do well now, having been literally plucked from the grave. The other lad has gone back to England already, not a whit the worse for his pint of blood! It only proves how all our emotions are products of our metabolism; and how a saint might very well be turned into a crusty old cynic by a short course of dyspepsia!

Went a day or two ago to Etaples to the Concentration Camp from which men are sent direct to the trenches. It was a perfectly fascinating place, the very apotheosis of order, activity, and dreariness. It's just like a Biblical picture; thousands of tents pitched in the driest of grey sand, not a blade of grass or a green leaf anywhere, and running right into a corner of it is the railway line itself.

As I was there, about 500 Scotch troops

E

were going off; and I have never seen anything like the picture of physical fitness they made, drawn up with their full fighting kit on, and standing like rocks under the blazing sun while the C.O. of the Depot gave the last final orders to the officer in charge. Then, when the word was given they swung perfectly into columns and marched out of the gate. All the other men who had not been ordered off were gathered round to give them a send off, and the chaff and ragging that went on was splendid. " Put some meat into it this time," and " None of that skulking now, that we've heard so much of;" and to one small thick-set lad like a fully-loaded shire horse with his square red knees and broad back—" You'll never get one of them Boches, Sandy, they tell me they can't 'arf run !" All as cheery as boys, except the officers, who looked as though they were convinced they had lost something and would think of it later on.

Coming back, we passed by the training

camp, where the men are taught actual trench warfare. There is a miniature battlefield laid out with English and German trenches, communication trenches, machine gun emplacements and every detail complete. Here they are taught every item likely to form a part of their future career, from going down into the communication trench, mounting the firing step, bayoneting imaginary Germans in the shape of bags of straw, to being carried down in stretchers by the R.A.M.C. men from the front line trench. I stood and watched them for some time and it was perfectly thrilling.

This morning after breakfast I heard singing in the street and going to the window saw the 17-year-old class going to join up. They made a fine show, four abreast, with an old poilu at the rear; and they swung down the village street with quite an inspiring air, singing some patriotic song with a verve and go that was splendid to hear.

As they went by, a poor drunken fellow came out of a café with an accordion. He had been called up, too, and wore his pitiable little bunch of tricolour and tinsel on his chest; and from sheer force of habit he started in to wring the Marseillaise out of his ruin of an instrument. He was a gawky, loose-lipped lad of about nineteen, very drunk and very dishevelled, and did not make a really martial figure, standing there in the bright morning sun with his high collar and stained bow tie. He will be very tired of that tune and all its associations before he is back in mufti again.

My old seagull is no end better, and sits on his bit of rockery in the garden looking as surly and aggressive as only a really healthy seagull can. It quite cheers me up to see him waggle his head and swallow when anyone comes too near. I think he knows me, too, for he looks very keenly at me and makes quaint little gurgling noises in his throat, but does not seem scared when I talk to him.

We have had Zeppelins over here recently, but no bombs dropped. I suppose they pass near here on their way to England; but they plunge us into total darkness all night, and we have to read by candles and get around with an " Orilux " as best we can.

I go out most evenings on the Plage now after dinner, and talk French with a delightful little thing I met bathing. It's certainly the best way to learn the language, and she seems a willing teacher. She's the epitome of everything French and feminine—Margot by name.

Last night we had Zeps. again, and heavy firing for some time from the batteries near here. Nothing was hit, however, as far as I know, and no bombs dropped.

Heavy convoy early this morning, 42 men and ten officers. Bathed in morning, heavy sea running, and Margot got out of her depth, shipped a lot of water and went down. She swims well, but seemed incapable of even walking when I pulled her into shallow water, so I had to carry her up to her hut.

Great sensation on shore; but I honestly believe the whole thing was a wheeze on her part, for she did it so neatly and opportunely and lay so gracefully in my arms. They're a quaint crowd here!

Glorious day to-day, high wind blowing and sea lovely. Bathed, and Margot turned up fresh as paint again, so I am convinced it was a plant now.

Had very few cases through yesterday and got to bed early.

Another day of absolutely nothing to do. Sat on the beach all day, and heard extremely heavy firing all morning which seemed to come from the English coast. Bathed several times before lunch, and lay in sun the rest of the morning and talked to Margot.

—— came to lunch and we had a very cheery time till three, when we again went on the beach and lay and bathed.

PART II

I GOT orders to join this ambulance a day or two ago and came direct up the line by car, since a Colonel was good enough to give me a lift.

My billet is priceless; I sometimes lie in my valise and smile at the sheer grotesqueness of it all. Here am I, a ratepayer of the Borough of Westminster, in my bed; and with me in the same room are ten other gentlemen, a quantity of mud-soaked straw for our beds to rest on, guttering candles and a smell like a damp grave. Mud is simply everywhere; there is a terrible draught, and still an impression of no air prevails. We laugh at the feeblest jokes, drink—out of tin mugs— whiskey and chlorinated water which has a subtle taste of death in it, and smoke incessantly. Yet it's a fascinating life, and

56

I am very happy here; I frankly can't imagine how or why!

It is really impossible to give the least idea of the country here, the desolation and destruction simply beggars description. For at least eight miles round where I am now there is not a stone building of any sort or kind left, and practically not a tree. There are a few gaunt wild-armed things here and there, all shell-smashed and chipped, and these just make the country all the more dreary. The hill sides are pocketed with great shell holes, and the roads are constantly being renewed as fast as they are shelled to bits.

This morning and afternoon I went a most fascinating tour with my Colonel, of all the new ground we have just taken; and the state there is even more awful than here. The entire country is so shell-scarred that you honestly could not lay a table-cloth down anywhere at all without covering a hole. Dead bodies everywhere, men and horses lying like sleepy children, side by side and limbs asprawl ; and since the enemy only left here two days ago the novelty and realism has not worn off, and they are still men and still horses, and not just bloated heaps of skin and clothes, like those farther back. Hands and legs stick out in the most uncanny way from heaps of earth and sandbags, and in the wind which flutters their muddy sleeves they almost seem to be waving a greeting or calling for help. Gangs of men are busy burying them, and in a few days they will be left quiet, until they come in the path of a new road or trench, when they will be dismembered as a gardener removes the outer roots of a tree, leaving the rest intact. We were having our sandwiches in our present front line trench when a man came along to tell us that someone had been sniped round the corner. We took about thirty strides round a heap of sandbags, and there he lay in the mud of the fire step, just quietly dying. He was a big strapping fellow about 30 years of age, with a skin

like a girl's and fair crisp hair ; and as he
lay there with his brown leather jerkin on
he reminded me irresistibly of one of Robin
Hood's men—somehow he looked English
to his nails. He had been having his lunch,
and had stood up to look round, and the
Boche had got him neatly through the
head behind the ears. He was quite un-
conscious, and the blood which ran from
his nose and mouth made him breathe in
a horribly snoring, bubbling way. One
had a painful wish that he would spit and
clear his throat, or blow his nose, or something. He died while we stood round him
with our sandwiches in our hands ; and in
thirty strides we were round into our own
little bay again and the Regimental M.O.
was cutting his disc off and getting him
taken away.

I saw a quaint thing, too, just before
lunch. We had pushed on into a part
whence the enemy has gone but which is
not yet consolidated, and as we walked
along there was a queer little noise like a

violin string breaking, and an officer next to me said : " There's some devil sniping us." I said, " Oh, I wondered what it was ! " and also wondered what had happened to my stomach that made me feel as if my lunch had gone wrong. I did not, however, mention this to the officer! In a minute or two, we, or rather one of the N.C.O.'s with us, localized the place where this firing was coming from, and a party was told off to rout them. The sniping party was in a sort of mixed clump of trees; so an N.C.O. and two men started to double over the open towards them, taking two Lewis guns with them. When they were about three hundred yards from the clump of trees, three men ran out and made across the open for a more sheltered spot, whereupon our lads opened fire on them with their Lewis. One man went down immediately, just rolling over like a shot rabbit. I thought in fact he had put his foot in a hole and would be up again instantly, it looked so like a stumble. The other ran about thirty yards, dodging like a snipe, and had almost reached a big heap of sandbags and mud when he suddenly did what looked like a stage death. He fell down, and his rifle jerked out of his hand. He then staggered to his feet again, ran about ten yards *towards us,* and then simply jumped into the air and dropped in a heap. As we walked back, I was told that the Boches frequently leave behind one or two stout fellows like that to do as much harm as they can before the inevitable end, so as to hold up the occupation of new land. I shall never forget that sight as long as I live. It was my first experience of " walking up " men like hares, and it seemed incredible that no one protested. So much for civilisation !

Brewery Redoubt. Maricourt.

Things have been very quiet this last few days: it has been largely a question of consolidating our gains and repairing roads, etc ; and of course there have been comparatively few casualties and not much for us to do in our line. I have spent my time wandering around our line seeing things—I have never had such material to observe in my life. It's all wonderful, and all new to me.

I was walking in a field near a battery to-day and was looking at some old gun-pits when a shell pitched in the next field, making a noise like a big paper bag being burst, and throwing up a huge cloud of earth. While I stood looking another one came, making such a quaint eerie scream-ing noise, and dropped right into a trench full of men in my field. There was a terrific "whoof," and then—just like a clown in the pantomime—a man shot up into the air and dropped, arms and legs all sprawl-ing, at least ten yards off. While I was walking across to him his own battery M.O. came up out of his dug-out and some stretcher-bearers picked him up and

carried him along to his aid post. The
M.O. and I went and looked into the
trench where he'd come from, and found
another poor chap with his foot blown off,
quite conscious and apparently in very
little pain. The stretcher-bearers carried
him away, too, and as it wasn't my business I didn't like to stay; so that was the
last I saw of it. They only fired those
two shells into that field; and in two
minutes the men were out again walking
round and grooming the horses, and
the whole incident apparently forgotten.
That's the amazing part out here. An
accident like that in England would draw
a crowd of three hundred people for half
an hour. Here it's over and forgotten in
five minutes after its occurrence.

There is a good deal of shelling going
on all the time; but it's quite local, so
that you can walk along a road and see
a battery being shelled in the next field
and still be really quite safe except for
stray shots. I had heard that before I

came up, but I really never believed it till now.

There are some of these men out here who really have no fear whatever, or really put no value whatever on their life. I was told to-day of an Irish Sergeant in one regiment who is like that. We are still pushing into new ground, and there are plenty of Die-hards left behind to snipe, and this man's method is as follows. He takes four men at dawn and posts them so that they can see a large area of country. Then, after daylight, he strolls around in the open in likely places, and is, of course, sniped to some certainty by one or more of the Boche. He then retires to his trench and waits for the return of his observation men, who are always able to give him the location of the sniper, whereupon our friend takes the usual steps to exterminate him. He has been doing this every day since I came and has made many bags, but it implies a recklessness which is to my mind almost insane!

64

It is a perfectly terrible sight to cross this ground newly won from the Germans, with men lying just where they fell, some in definite lines where a machine gun caught them, and others in little groups of isolated men, where shell or bullet hit them. One man I saw to-day had a whole story to tell. He had evidently been rushing a trench, and got a bullet through the stomach about twenty yards from his objective. He had thrown away his rifle at once and crawled to a shell hole for cover, and here I found him. He had undone his trousers and pulled up his shirt to see the wound, and died as he looked at it; for he lay there, his two hands holding his dirty shirt up to show a clean red hole in his muddy skin and, with his head fallen forward on his chest, he seemed even now to be wondering just what to do next!

F

I was fired on deliberately and individually to-day for the first time, and it gives you such a strange, cold, furious desire to hit back, it was curious to realise it afterwards. I was going up to my advance dressing station with my orderly when a Boche aeroplane came over. The orderly said : " That's a Boche, sir," and I said " Oh ! " and looked up with quite a kindly feeling for the airman, he made such a pretty picture against the blue cloud-flecked sky. All at once he dived down at us and I heard his machine gun making a noise like a riveter's hammer, and bullets started to " phit, phit ! " all round us. " Here's a dug-out, sir," said the orderly, and we darted about ten yards up the road and in like a couple of startled rabbits. It seemed almost inconceivable that anyone should go out of his way to fire on two individuals like that, and the thing which made one literally boil was the impotence which forced one to run to earth like a rat. If that Boche had descended then from engine trouble, I should have strangled him gladly, having no other weapons, and the Geneva convention could have gone to Hell ! How true, as the Bishop of London says, this war is undoubtedly uplifting us !

We have been having glorious weather this last few days, quite sunny and warm. If they would only stop shelling it would be really pleasant living here !

PART III

WITH A BATTALION

(AUTHOR'S NOTE : The Diary of the first few months of my life with the Battalion was unfortunately lost in an accident which overtook my aid post on one occasion.

We were out of the line most of the time however, and it was mainly a record of quiet days spent in the most delightful company, and personal sketches of those officers and men who were to make of my stay with that Battalion such a period of real happiness for me. It was therefore scarcely suitable for publication in any case.)

We moved to-day from Ville to Wardeques, leaving at midnight. A lovely moon was shining, and the Battalion looked like a great dusky caterpillar along the white

68

road, the stretchers carried by the company stretcher-bearers giving an added effect of horns along the creature's back. A glorious night and a wonderful experience, half the men being hidden sometimes in a misty hollow, while the rest swung steadily along in the cold white light on higher ground. Took train to Arques at 2.15 a.m. and had an amusing if trying journey. The heat was appalling; but Corporal Orris served his usual wonderful breakfast and we were a very cheery party in our carriage.

Four really happy days in Wardesques, a charming little village. In camp, but Battalion Headquarters is in a very good house, kept by a lady and her daughter ; daughter very pretty and kindly. Had plenty to do training bearers, as we hear we are to go to Ypres very soon now. Went to Divisional sports one day, where our

Divisional General addressed us. He said,
" I want to say how pleased I have been
with your bayonet fighting to-day" (our
Sergeant won the Instructing prize). You
are out here for one purpose only—to kill
Boches. From what I have seen every
man here is good for two or three Boches.
That's what I want. You all of you put
any amount of viciousness and beef into
your work to-day, with no fancy work.
That's what I want. I only have to say
that I have always been proud to command
this Division. I am prouder than ever
now. Also that you may have an oppor-
tunity of showing very soon what you can
do against the real thing in the open !—
(Cries from hundreds of men " That's
what we want ! ")

Left billets at 7.30 a.m. and had a
most loving farewell from the daughter at
H.Q. I said (trying to be nice and get
away, though she looked very attractive
leaning out of her window in her plain
linen nightdress with a blue scarf tied

round her fair hair)—" Comme c'est triste de partir. Je ne peux pas vous dire comme je suis triste." It was a lovely morning, we were moving to new ground, she made an awfully pretty picture and I was really rather happy. She put her little hand up to her trembling wet mouth and cried : " Vous dites que vous etes triste, et vous riez. Mon Dieu, vous Anglais ! " and let her blind fall, giving me a quick moist kiss as it dropped on my head !

Wormhoudt.

Had a charming march here under a blazing sun, and the men did magnificently, scarcely one falling out. They were in splendid spirits and full of jokes and laughter. It is really a pleasure to be with them.

We passed another Battalion on the road, with a little covered buggy bringing up the rear of their transport—they had found it somewhere and were using it as a mess cart. Its incongruity struck many of our fellows and raised a good deal of chaffing ; and one man, with that genius for the apt phrase which distinguishes the Cockney, shouted " Now then ! this way ! Bushey Park ! Hampton Court, just about to start ! "—the whole in that hoarse staccato voice typical of touts for such vehicles !

On another occasion, during a halt, one or two of the men got ragging and strayed on to the road, which is contrary to march discipline. A young officer, newly out, shouted to an N.C.O. " Sergeant, keep those men off the road, I can't have them playing indiscriminately like that." I was sitting in the ditch with the rest, and heard one thin-faced humourist say to his mate in the arch tones of a shocked spinster " Oh, I sye, did you ever 'ear such lang-widge."

He imagined no one heard, but it delighted me !

Most of the way I rode with the transport officer, who has been through the country before in the early days of the war, and was full of interesting little anecdotes.

He is by way of being a sort of Marathon Don Juan ; and most of his reminiscences are like farces in this—a bedroom scene invariably figures in them somewhere. But he gave me one delightful sidelight on his character. He pointed me out a heap of bricks off the road, formerly a château where he had been billeted in 1914, and, " the most wonderful billet I ever was in, Doc, I never had such a time in my life," he said. I waited confidently for some preternaturally Rabelaisian story, and then, " They had the most adorable pair of Cocker spaniels there, and we used to have great times in the woods together," said he, and launched out into a glowing description of their cunning ways and charms.

After a while, and obviously strictly in order of their importance in his memory, " There were two daughters, too, quite unique women "—and we were back on the old topic again.

This is a largish dull town with no great charm of any sort. I was billeted in a very charming house with very delightful people, obviously well-to-do, and had a gorgeous time. —— and —— got a billet with two girls and an Aunt in, and hoped for great things. They asked me to go in after dinner and talk, as neither of them talks French ; and we had much champagne and a very cheery evening. I could see nothing was coming to either of them, so told them so, and went off to bed. Talked for a while with my host, hostess and daughter, and got up next morning to find flowers in my room, and a note asking me to breakfast with the family, and not to go across to H.Q. The hour being 6.30 a.m. I was amazed to find them all three up, and we had a very charming meal together. They had poached four eggs for me, being English, and themselves drank coffee and played with bread. The old lady was very interested to hear about my dog at home, and kissed me on leaving and said "Bonne chance, gosse " like a mother —the old man was much amused.

Van Biezom area, near Poperinghe.
Marched to our new camp to-day. A terrible day, a blazing sun and no wind, and the men right up against it for heat. The last four miles was a nightmare, men falling out every now and again, and my ghastly job being to fall on them and bully, cajole, and bluff them to their feet again. We did wonderfully well however ; for although plenty of men fell out, I got every man up again on his feet, and every man finished except four, whom I had to send to hospital on ambulances with exhaustion. They are wonderful fellows, with heart enough for ten each.

We are in Armstrong huts here, and go into the line again in three days. There is any amount to do, and to-morrow the Colonel is taking me round the trenches we are to take over. I am dead beat so I shall clear to bed.

The camp was bombed by a Boche plane last night ; and between our archies and their bombs there was very little sleep for an hour or two. No casualties.

Went for a tour round Elverdinghe defences with the Colonel, and had a very interesting day. The village is pretty badly knocked about, the men living entirely in dug-outs. The château is curiously un-touched—untouched in comparison, of course—and is being used as a mess by artillery. We ate our sandwiches in a ruined farmhouse, and then walked down to where we had left our horses. As we reached them the Boche began to shell the road, and put about a dozen over in quick succession. Nothing hit us, however, the nearest being about fifty yards away in a field on our left.

Rode via Poperinghe, which is curiously dead-alive; dead inasmuch as all the windows are broken and boarded up; and alive—with Tommies. Saw one really pretty girl in a narrow cobbled street, slovenly and rather dirty as all Belgians are, but with an astonishing richness of colour, and a smile like a window in Heaven. The old women, of whom there are large numbers, all pendulous-breasted and with bare and dusty feet and legs, work incessantly at lace-making which they do on a frame like an old-fashioned saddle. The threads are tied to small spindles or bobbins, and they throw them nimbly backwards and forwards at lightning speed, so making the pattern. They make rather a quaint picture with their fat stupid faces and deft fingers, working ceaselessly away in some by-lane of this dreary town, which is shelled regularly once every few days. Got back to camp to find a concert party on, and after that had dinner.

Roussel Farm.

Moved up here last night, the battalion coming through without losing a man.

The Boche was shelling the village very heavily with 5.9's as we approached, looking for a gun just to the left of it, and there was some anxiety as to his switching off suddenly on to the village itself. The shell-bursts here are really pretty. The earth is a lovely brown, and the huge spouts of bright brown earth showing in the evening sun through the green trees make a wonderful show. The noise was pretty considerable, however, and great trees were going up like matches, so we were all very glad to get down below.

I have got a very good spot, quite dry and recently concreted over, so one ought to get no rats in it. Most charming of all is a swallow's nest in the roof corner, for I can lie and watch the two little creatures bringing in food-stuff, and going through all their domestic routine with that happy earnestness which distinguishes birds. It's wonderful how little they mind the noise; and only sometimes, when something big drops really near and jars you like a slap in the face, do they leave the nest and flutter twittering round.

Did not get much sleep last night, for there is a 6-in. naval gun in a field next to the camp, which shakes the earth every time he goes off. As this occurred every minute or so for about two hours, one's head felt as though a giant had been boxing one's ears for the same space of time.

Went up into the front line this morning with the Colonel, and had a very interesting trip. The trenches are so different from those of the Somme, being deep in grass and poppies on either side, and all the fields in full bloom with flax and poppies, too. There was a good deal of shelling going on, mainly counter battery work though, so it was only odd shells which came near us. The Boche got one of our balloons about 3 p.m., and it was a wonderful thing to see it burst suddenly into flames and come down like a big red cloud of smoke. I never saw the observers jump, so I imagine they were both killed in it.

Had a bad night last night with dysentery—this heat and shortage of water are, of course, responsible ; but I feel like a chewed rag this morning. We were heavily bombed by planes, too, which did not help any. There were an enormous number of planes over all day, and one or two Boche ones, the latter trying to spot a 1.11-in. gun which is placed near us. It's a fascinating thing to see them being chased by ours, and shelled by our archies. All the talk is of the " push," and there is now no doubt we are to be in it. I heard to-day in confidence that we had been chosen as one Battalion to go over, and that it would be pretty soon.

Last night—between periods of intense intestinal activity—I whiled away the time by composing the following doggerel, suggested by the various ways I have heard the name of our village pronounced.

" ELVERDINGHE as you like it."

or

" WHAT'S IN A NAME."

Dear little place !
  How sad that we have met
When with your people's tears
  Your eyes are wet !
How sweet you must have been
When in your fields of green
Your children sang,
  And Peace—your gentle Queen—
Ruled Elverdang !

81

G

Now, in your quiet streets,
   Chaos supreme !
There, o'er those tortured trees,
   Very-lights gleam.
Hark ! At your old church door
Shells scream and cannons roar,
   Shrill bugles ring !
Ah ! Now you smile no more,
   War ! Elverding !

Yet how sweet to think that soon,
   When the war is over,
Boys and girls will laugh and sing
   In your fields of clover !
Lovers walk your lanes among
   Sighing, panting, clingy—
How your heart will throb for them,
   Tender Elverdinghy !

Yet I think, dear, you were truest
   When I saw you first.
Sun at hottest, sky at bluest,
   I afire with thirst !
Then I thought as Tommy thinks
   When he's wet and muddy,
And I murmured, 'twixt my drinks,
   This indeed is Bloody.

So far the war has produced no stranger
phenomenon—than that I should embark
on poetic outpourings. Possibly an exten-
sion of the Dysentery !

I went out to see the Sergeant-Major putting a new draft through their drill, and was much amused for a time. The first and most important thing for them to grasp is that they represent an inefficiency entirely unique ; and this impression is conveyed to them by the simple method of making them do everything at least ten times, under a running fire of criticism and withering sarcasm. Finally, one man, having endeavoured on five occasions to get his thumb (or little finger, I forget which) into the precise angle laid down by King's Regs., and having failed lamentably—nay, disgustingly—to conform to the Sergeant - Major's standard, was ordered to repeat the manœuvre yet another time. " My God," said he under his breath, but not far enough under to escape his mentor. " Don't let me 'ear you use that name on the parade ground again," roared he. " God made you, but God knows who had the drillin' of you, for I don't. If I 'ear you say that again, you're for the Guard Room, my lad. Now then, as you were ! "

This without the flicker of a smile from anyone, and with a ferocity and intentness which chills the blood. It was too much for me, and I blew my nose discreetly and moved on.

In the evening the heat was intense, a heavy thundery feeling in the air, and not a breath of wind.

We left Roussel Farm at 10 p.m. for Blouet Farm, and completed the relief without a hitch.

A very fascinating trip up to the new line, and I should have revelled in it had I not felt so thoroughly done up. "Very lights" were everywhere, and as the Boche evidently suspected something, there was a good deal of shelling, too.

Everything else dead quiet. All one heard was an occasional sharp challenge

from a sentry, the staggering crash of a
bursting crump near by, and apart from
that only the steady croaking of millions
of frogs, and the soft pad, pad of feet in
the dusty road.

It was pitch dark when we struck the
communication trench—and to walk in
single file along it was like a walk blindfold
through a conservatory. Every few yards
a new scent hit your nostrils, every flower
being forced to give its utmost on a damp
hot night like that ; and now and again
one would walk into sweetly cool patches,
delicately scented, and wonderfully still
and quiet. Altogether a charming walk.

Arrived to find Blouet Farm briskly
shelled, but I have a good aid post, and
was soon asleep.

Was called at 2.30 to look at six men of
a working party who had been caught by
a shell. Four were only slight, but two
were pretty bad. While I was dressing the
last, about 3.15 a.m., a Boche plane came
over very low, and being fired at by our

Lewis Gun section, he opened fire, too, in return. It was curious to hear the shrill scream of his bullets now and again, and hear one or two hit some piece of iron roofing like a riveter. Just then a big naval gun went off near us, and blew our candle out.

The Boche got away, and the last I saw of him was a big black dragon-fly against the blue black of the sky.

Last night we were shelled to hell between 2 a.m. and 4.30, and entirely due to a blithering idiot of a signaller who lit in his billet a fire of damp wood, the smoke of which was, of course, spotted by aeroplanes. Fortunately most of the shells went fifty yards to the left of the farm, but several dropped bang on the billets, and one or two men were hit. The noise was pretty steep, however, for the Boche has a new type of shell here which we never got on the Somme, and the crash it makes is incredible. One result of it is that there is a new grave just opposite our H.Q. mess, and several good fellows have gone down the line maimed for life. I heard they put a battery out of action in the next field to us.

We hear that there are to be an enormous number of guns put along the line of trees outside the farm, so that the push is evidently pretty close. One rather pleasing thing is that they shelled Brigade H.Q. to such an extent that all had to take refuge in the dug-outs in the grounds. That cheers one, since the red-tabbed lads get little or nothing in the way of shelling, and are apt to forget what it's like.

At dawn our old friend the Boche plane turned up again. He never misses a day, and is certainly a plucky fellow, for every Lewis Gun and archie in the neighbourhood is turned loose on him ; and he flies pretty low, too. The battalion on our left

had a shell plumb into a dug-out at B.H.Q.
—killed five and wounded eight.

Last night was worse than the night
before—at least as far as I was concerned.
The road up which the transport comes at
night passes just behind my aid post, and
as the artillery had been using it during
the day to bring up ammunition, etc., the
Boche opened a barrage of 5.9's on it
at ten at night. At 10.45 our transport
arrived in the yard behind my aid post,
and I went out to see a man who was hit
by a splinter. The place was literally all
over bits of shrapnel, and I have never
seen limbers unloaded in such record time!
I was holding my water-bottle in my hand
as I came round the corner, and a piece of
shrapnel came past like a bullet and went
clean through the strap, cutting it in half
and puncturing the bottle. It was a won-

derful sight though, shells bursting all round and above the yard, and the horses in the limbers standing as quiet as on parade. They are the most wonderful beasts !

One shell pitched in a group of men and killed two and wounded thirteen, most only slightly. This evening I saw a paper saying a squadron of battle planes were to go up to-morrow morning after my lonely Boche, so there will be dirty work about 2.45 a.m. to-morrow.

Another very hot night ; we were shelled continuously from 10 o'clock till 2.30 by 5.9's and H.E. shrapnel. I had one or two cases pretty early on and was busy till midnight, but from then onwards it was just a case of sitting in your dug-out waiting to be hit. They were putting them literally all over us, so much so that it was no use trying to keep my dug-out door closed, and I could see them bursting all round and about like fireworks, the noise being simply incredible. I had two direct hits on my roof, fortunately both glancing ones, but the second of them made such a concussion inside that I was quite knocked out for a minute or two. It was the queerest sensation one could imagine, just as if the walls and roof had suddenly been concertinaed in by some means and then as suddenly pulled out again. It knocked all the stuff off my table, and fetched a great mass of sandbagging down the air shaft. We had several fellows hit in the billets round about, so I was pretty busy in the morning when dawn broke and the shelling stopped. As soon as it had quieted down, ——, who was with a Lewis Gun party in the field on the other side of the road waiting for the Boche plane, came over to see if I was all right. He had seen the two hits, he said, and they all thought the second one had gone plumb through.

The Boche never turned up ; I suppose it was too misty for him, for there was a fine rain falling at dawn, so I went back to bed at four and slept till nine, as very few were coming over by then.

Went to lunch at Brigade Headquarters with the C.O., but as the château was itself being shelled to hell by this time, we were both naturally anxious that it should clear up. By 12.30 rain had stopped and shelling decreased, so we set off for lunch. The trenches were really lovely after the rain, the grasses, flowers and poppies being simply perfect. It was very quaint to see the C.O.'s orderly marching along in front of us in his tin hat, carrying every death-dealing appliance possible on his person, and holding in one swinging hand at his side a bright crimson poppy just sparkling with rain. This war is really a grotesque business. There is simply no sense in it.

One thing I learned to-day is that we are going over the top in a month. I at once applied for leave. I'll not miss what may

be the last time I'll get in town without a
pretty good shot at it.

Last night was the quietest we have had
for some time ; there was a raid near
Ypres, and the Boche had all his guns
turned on that sector. I pushed off to bed
at 10.30 and slept like a log till 2.30, when
—— came in to say that he had been
blown over by a shell in Railway Trench
and would I give him something to make
him sleep. I could tell from his manner
that he wanted really to talk to someone
for a bit, so I got my servant to make some
cocoa and we sat and talked for an hour
or so.

It must have been a pretty close call for
all of them, for the shell pitched on the
traverse just next to them. He cleared off
much steadier about four o'clock, and I
slept again till nine. It rained on and off
all day. Started my trench tour about

10.30 and had a very wet trip. Called in and had a drink on No. 3 Coy, and —— told me a pigeon had been seen to fly out of Dead Man Wood, and make straight for the Boche lines. He has posted two of his professional murderers in the wood to-day, and to-night or so we may have the lad responsible for it.

My bearer Sergeant told me he was gassed during his trip down the line last night, and had to wear his mask for the whole journey. I should detest gas in a trench, it's like a rat in a trap—a rotten death. The —— had a few men killed yesterday, one being blown to pieces. The men picked him up and put him in sand-bags, and laid him out to be buried, afterwards going on with their work of repairing the parados. When the Padre came to bury him he found that by accident a bag of earth had been substituted for a bag of humanity, and half the parados had to be taken down before the mistake could be rectified. While I was at No. 3 Coy, ——

showed me where a 5.9 had dropped bang in the middle of his working party of thirty men the night before. By the grace of God it was a dud, or he and many of his men would have been cold this morning.

An intelligence report has just come in, saying there are to be two raids on the enemy line to-night at 11.30, both by the —— division and both, therefore on our right. Let's hope they keep the Boche busy again, and then we may have another quiet night.

I have had no casualties to-day.

Went a tour of the front line this afternoon with ——, and got caught in a heavy storm. As I have only one suit up here, I had to lie naked in my blanket and Burberry till my servant had dried the shirt and breeches—or more or less dried them.

The transport officer came up for dinner from the transport and we had a very

cheery meal. He delighted me by telling
me that his heartburn (entirely due to
alcohol, and for which I have been pre-
scribing Bismuth) has got so bad that he
now has to take two Bismuths before he
can stand a whiskey and soda—it stings so
going down.

Last night the shelling was a devil again,
and got so bad finally that the Colonel
telephoned the Brigade for some counter
battery work by our artillery. This was
given us, and towards 3.50 the Boche let
up a bit. I had a very busy night. A
number of our men were wounded and
killed, and I got all the gunners' wounded
to look after, too, since their M.O. (wise
fellow) was back with his Battery headquarters. They had no stretchers up
either; and I had to go out wandering
about the gun-pits in the open—a most
unpleasant business under the circum-

stances. One gunner dug-out got a direct hit and two men were killed and three wounded. One man was so shattered that it was almost impossible at first to tell how many men there were in the heap of flesh and clothes under the sandbags, and it was only by asking the survivors that one could be sure. Another dug-out had a shell clean through it from corner to corner, which burst finally just outside. It smashed one man's hand as it went through, but it hurt no one else. After I had finished them off, I went back to my place and lay down again, leaving my candle lit ; and I hadn't been there ten minutes when an H.E. shrapnel burst on the roof and the concussion blew the candle out and fetched about a hundredweight of sandbags down just inside the door. I thought at first I was buried and the door blocked ; but, after putting in about five minutes' pretty strenuous work bag shifting, I met my dear old bearer Sergeant also bag shifting from the outside, and all was well. He told me, with his usual courteous smile that he thought I was done for when he saw the roof in, and like a good fellow he walked round from his own place to dig me out, which was no pleasant business under the circumstances. I had a very curious instance of human nature later on. A gunner sergeant, a D.C.M., and obviously a pretty stout fellow, was brought in crying and making a devil of a fuss. I got him down and found he had been hit by a beam in his dug-out when it was blown in. His hip was badly bruised, but no bones were broken and nothing really the matter with him. But he kept shouting : " Oh ! mind my leg ! " and " Can't you do something for the pain ? " and generally making an ass of himself, till I told him if he didn't keep quiet, I'd have his stretcher put outside in the open. That quietened him, and I started to look at the others. The aid post was pretty full of wounded at the time, and only one candle going, but I flashed my torch around

H

and saw one of our own men sitting on a form quietly and upright, but looking like death. I thought he'd best be seen to first. He was only a boy, certainly not more than 22, and when we cut his jacket off he had a hole in his shoulder you could have put your hands into. He talked to me all the time I was dressing him, and told me the whole story : "We were comin' back from a fatigue up Railway Trench when they started putting them all round us. One or two of us was hit, and we got all crowded up in the trench, so I called out 'What's to be done, Corporal?' Someone shouted : ' Corporal's done in,' so I stood and waited for the trench to get clear again. Then one burst right on the traverse next to me and I got this in the shoulder. Then Ritchings, my right-hand man, shouted to me : ' We'd best get out of this,' so we started shovin' a bit and got clear and came down here. There's an Irishman lying outside here in the road, too. I think he's dead."

He said all this in the most matter-of-fact way, and was a perfectly amazing contrast to the Sergeant, who was still whimpering away in his corner.

My Bearer Sergeant is priceless on these occasions. He is entirely unaffected by shelling, and walks round usually with his tin hat on the back of his neck like a sunbonnet ; and to see him bandaging a man with a candle in the same hand as the bandage and spraying grease in every direction is a perfect treat to me. We got them all cleared off by about 4.30, and I went to bed and slept till 11, when my servant brought me some tea and biscuits, and a bright clean sun was pouring in through my door. It's always impossible to believe in the morning that one has had such a hell of a night. The country here is so green and full of flowers, and so quiet and peaceful in the mornings, that it is only by the new brown shell-holes and the colour of the water in my basin that I can believe that it really did take place.

Walked round the trenches after lunch and had a very interesting look through a sniper's post at the Boche lines.

Last night we were relieved by the ——s, and again the shelling was pretty bad. One of our men was killed about eleven o'clock in Bridge Street, and they sent him down to be buried. I had him put in my dug-out while the grave was being made, and then came the business of the burial service. Padre had gone down ahead to get cocoa and stuff ordered for us when we arrived, so the job had to be done by the second in command. We had no prayer book and no one knew the service, so we decided to have the Lord's Prayer read, and then I wrote out a little bit about " committing thy servant's body to the earth in the hope of a glorious resurrection hereafter " . . . was very nervous, and kept saying : " I'll mess the whole thing, I know damned well I will," and "Now let's see if I know the

Lord's Prayer all through; if I get that right it will be something." He rehearsed the other little bit at least ten times. We were all sitting round the table in Headquarters, and I could not help thinking how incredibly grotesque the whole business was. Four men solemnly hearing the Lord's Prayer rehearsed, like children learning a lesson. Finally, when —— was rapidly getting chaotic, there was a knock on the door and the Drill Sergeant showed his 6 ft. 4 under a steel helmet, saluted, and said in his usual parade-ground voice: " Pte. Edwards, E., ready for burial, sir, please." No one noticed the amazing phrasing, and we all tramped out. They had dug his grave behind Btn. H.Q., where the light couldn't be seen by the Boche, and already Pte. Edwards, in his ground sheet, had been lowered into the hole. The men stood round at attention, just the four diggers and Drill Sergeant, and then —— took off his tin hat and started in the most toneless voice imaginable to repeat his lesson. He did it just like a little child, putting no feeling into the words whatever, came to a full stop at the end as though there were more to come he had forgotten, and finally saved the situation by saying " Amen " in an equally flat and meaningless voice. Then we all put on our tin hats again, saluted, and filed off up the duck boards, leaving the fatigue party to fill in the grave. I looked back as we left them, and it made an amazing scene—the dull moon behind heavy rain-clouds just showing the stooping figures of the men at their work, back of them the flash of our guns, and over and around them every now and again the blaze of bursting shrapnel.

———'s first words on getting in were : " That went off all right, Doc, didn't it ? I thought I had messed it at one time, but I put in that ' Amen,' and I don't think the men noticed it." I assured him it had passed off very well, and we sat down to wait for the relieving battalion to arrive and take over. We had one or two men

102

brought in before we left who had been hit coming down Bridge Street, and we got away ourselves at about 12.15. The walk back was exciting, as they were suspicious there was a relief on and shelled the communication trench pretty heavily, but we had no casualties and got in to Roussel Farm about two o'clock.

Cocoa was ready, and eggs and bacon, and we had a really good meal. All the way coming down we had been saying what a treat it would be to get to bed and know there would be no shelling; and the first thing the transport officer started to talk about when we got there was that they had had several shells in the transport lines that night, that the leave train had been hit in Poperinghe Station, and that our billets had been shelled at intervals, too! We were all a bit irritable, and someone said : " Look here, we've heard enough about shelling ; it's all very well for you, but we've had enough shelling to last us a bit, and I don't want to hear any more about it. As far as I know, they don't shell this place at all, so for God's sake keep quiet."

The transport officer looked angry, and there was an uncomfortable silence; when, just like a stage effect, we all heard the well-known overhead-train noise of an approaching shell. Nobody said anything, but it was useless to ignore it, so I said: " How restful the wind sounds in the trees, doesn't it, sir ? " and turned towards the C.O. He roared with laughter, someone said, "I'm sorry, ——, have a drink?" and the whole thing passed off all right. We got to bed and there was a bit of shelling, but nothing bad or near, and I slept solid till eleven this morning. At that hour the Adjutant came in and said: "Here's something for you. You've got to get back to your aid post to relieve the ——'s M.O., who's sick." I took the paper with a bitter curse, opened it, and found I had got my leave, and was to start on the 24th—*to-morrow* !

Saw a balloon brought down to-day by a Boche plane, and the two observers descend in their parachutes, swinging in the high wind till it made you sick to look at them.

PART IV.

CAME by train from the base, after having spent two very charming days at Boulogne.

Caught the leave train at midnight, and slept in it till 4 a.m., when it left, having six a side in 2nd class carriages. A fearful journey, like a nightmare honeymoon— one's legs all tangled with everyone else's, and one's neck feeling like a corkscrew. Got out at Hazebrouk feeling like death, and determined to get a car of some sort for the rest of the journey. Had an omelette at the Hotel Faucon, the daughter of the house being very kindly disposed, and then struck an R.A.M.C. man whom I knew. We talked a while and he finally put me to Poperinghe in a car. Went on by lorry and found the Battalion in rest. Had a very pleasant reception, the place feeling quite like home again.

Heard we had rather heavy casualties in

the line during my absence, my locum
saying he had a lot of work. He also had
a direct hit on his aid post in the line,
which must have been very unpleasant.
Glad I missed it ! The ——s had their
M.O. killed, too, and on the whole the line
is pretty brisk apparently.

Heard more details of our share in the
coming big push, which is certainly going
to be some " show," and the air is full of
preparation for it.

Got to bed early, as I was dead tired,
and slept like a log.

Saw sick at 7.30. Went out afterwards
to see our Battalion rehearse the show, and
had a very interesting day. I am starting
a series of first-aid lectures to all companies in turn, so that every man may, if
necessary, act efficiently as a bearer.

I can't help feeling there is so little one
can do to take one's part in a show like

this. The men depend on you so awfully; and their job is so much more difficult and hard to bear than mine. However, one can only do one's best and try and think out little things which may help.

Saw some charming orders to-day. There is a machine for signalling called a "Flapper;" and orders were circulated to the effect that a Divisional Signalling Officer would attend to-morrow to give a lecture on the use of the "Flapper." I would give a good deal to hear the comments of the men on that.

Had another rehearsal of the attack to-day, and again everything passed off excellently. The barrage is imitated by the drums, and is in a way very realistic.

The M.O. of the ——s, who are in the line now, was killed to-day by a shell on his aid post. "There, but for the Grace of God, goes your humble servant."

The ——s had a number of men gassed
in the line to-day also. How I detest gas.
I suppose everybody is scared of something, and mine's gas, that's all.

A quiet day. A band came and played
in camp in the evening, and it was quite
sentimental to hear them playing all the
airs so redolent of London, and know that
not a quarter of the men listening there
would ever see London again.

Heard a very quaint thing to-day on the
road leading past the Camp. It was raining steadily, as it can do here, and the road
was a perfect quagmire in consequence,
churned into an average two feet of greasy
mud by two never-ending streams of traffic.
A G.S. wagon had got ditched, and the
driver had expended at least ten minutes
of blood and tears trying to get the wheel
out, and all to no avail. Other drivers—
in that effort to be ingenious which char-

acterises all drivers of all vehicles—trying
to get past him, had themselves become
wedged ; and by the time I arrived the
whole road was one heaving, sweating
chaos of horses and vehicles. The original
delinquent had climbed on his box again
and was making one last frenzied effort to
get his horses away, when suddenly upon
the scene appears the A.P.M., very brisk
and very efficient on his mud-splashed
chestnut thoroughbred. "Now, then,
what's all this about? " says he; and then,
catching sight of our sweating, mud-
soaked friend bouncing like a marionette
on his box—" Here, you, what the devil's
the use of sitting up there doing nothing ?
Get down and do some work, man, get
down and do some work." There is a tense
silence while the driver eyes him from his
eyrie, the rain pouring in a steady stream
off his hat, and then : " Well, my blinkin'
eart's broke ! " says he, and throwing the
reins on his horses' backs, continues to
stare hopelessly into the distance. The

whole scene was so intensely comic that it cheered me up for the day !

Talked a lot of rubbish in the evening to the old man and woman who own the farm here about being " fiancé " to the daughter, and great merriment prevailed in the kitchen, as we leave to-morrow. They would be surprised if they knew just to what extent their daughter is " fiancée " to most of the men in the Battalion—or most probably they would not be surprised at all, such is the outlook of the country folk here.

Marched to-day to Forest Area.

A hot sun but a cool wind, and the Battalion came through intact. We arrived at our new area about three o'clock, and met the 2nd ——s going out to rest. Their transport officer said they had been shelled out of the camp last night. As we are taking over their camp, this is, to say the least, not cheering. Heard that the ——s had heavy casualties last night in the line, losing four sergeants. The Boche put over many gas shells, too, so I must read up my memoranda on gas to-night.

As I sit here writing this before dinner in a lovely shady glade bathed in a golden sunset, a machine gun company is unpacking its mess stores across the pathway. One man has just undone a large hamper of food, and produced therefrom two wee kittens, who instantly fell upon each other and rolled in a fighting heap upon the grass. These men will keep pets under any circumstances.

Several shells have just dropped in the field next our wood, but no casualties that I could hear of. If there are any, they'll find me anyhow. The Headquarters are in three tents for to-night, and they are all of the real fishing-smack red canvas which, camouflaged with branches broken from trees, makes a perfectly entrancing sight. In fact, seen from here, under the green trees and in such a wonderful light as now prevails (a sort of golden green of incredible clarity) the men standing here and there in their khaki, with red burned arms and faces, the whole thing is like a Gaiety " set " more than anything else. I hope they don't shell us to-night; the transport is just next door, and I shall hate to see the horses torn up.

A shell has just dropped in the trees about fifty yards off, and a cloud of brown earth and canvas is still hanging in the air.

It is good to sit here, after a cold bath and a change, and watch our Mess Corporal getting dinner ready, and all the other activities of the camp going on as though in England. The men have made their little bivouacs under the trees and are sitting round smoking after their tea. The sky is a wonderful greenish grey now, with not a breath of wind ; and up in the far-off sky scores of planes move backwards and forwards, while every now and again Boche shrapnel bursts near the big still balloon which hangs so sleepily over us.

Last night we were shelled fairly heavily, but not so as to make us take to the "slits." I slept till three, when the noise was so great as to make sleep impossible except in snatches. This morning I went to see our Battalion do a practice raid across a canal dug to represent the real one, and a very interesting thing it was. The men, stripped from the feet to the waist, and looking like the members of a beauty chorus with their white shapely legs showing under their tunics, evidently enjoyed the show to the hilt. They have rolled up mats of wire and canvas which they unroll before them over the mud of the canal, and the whole thing passed off excellently. In the afternoon, the Battalion moved about a mile further up the line to our present area, arriving about five o'clock. We are in a farm house, and every hedge surrounding us is simply lined with guns. There is a poor cow here in a stall which was hit by shrapnel several days ago and has been entirely neglected by its owners, who only come each night to milk her. She is in a terrible state, and makes a perfectly heart-breaking picture, rocking herself on her poor weak legs, and swinging her tortured head from side to side in a way which nearly makes one cry. What a filthy business this war is, that even poor harmless beasts such as she must suffer because of it. I have swabbed her up pretty well to-night and she seems a good deal more easy already. Just before dinner the Boche began to shell us pretty briskly, and our guns started to reply. The noise was appalling all during dinner, and has grown worse since ; and as the bombardment starts in real earnest at 2 p.m. to-morrow, there will be no more real sleep worth speaking of for anyone until the show is over.

The sky is wonderfully clear and still, and the flashes of our guns and the splash of the bursting shells makes a perfectly beautiful picture. We do not go into the front line till the 20th, but one would be much better off there than here, since here we have no protection whatever against shell fire, and the Boche is certain to start searching for the guns which are all round us as soon as the bombardment begins. The Boche raided our lines last night, sending over two companies. Out of these 300 men only 6 reached our lines, the rest being caught by Lewis guns almost on their own parapet. These 6 caught one officer of the ——s and got off with him, the raid achieving nothing else.

A fairly quiet night, the Boche replying very little to our guns. The latter kept at it pretty well all night, however, so that sleep was hard to get. It rained all night in torrents, too, and my roof leaked steadily on to my head and body. On the whole a poor night.

As I moved dismally round the hut, trying to get at least the head of my valise under a dry place, the second in command, who was sharing the hut with me, woke up and said drowsily : " What's the matter, Doc ? " " I'm trying to get my head from under this damned shower bath," said I. " That's the worst of the professional classes," murmured he, " a finnicky crowd always," and dropped off again into dreamland.

That sent me to sleep happy !

The day opened clear but gusty, and we heard early on that our bombardment was put off till six a.m. to-morrow. Spent a very quiet day around the camp, the C.O. not wishing me to leave in case of casualties. It is very quaint to see the companies going through their gas drill with respirators on. They look most weird and sinister figures, marching slowly round in these hideous helmets like a body of murderers going on a raid. There was a bit of Boche shelling during the day, and our guns kept steadily at it after lunch, but nothing occurred in the way of casualties. It was very quaint too to sit in my chair outside my hut and listen to No 3's gramophone. Every time a shell burst really near, or one of our big guns went off, the concussion jarred the needle across the disc, so that it produced a most uncanny effect, as if the machine itself had been startled. Then the air would recommence quietly again.

I dressed my old cow again just now, and she is improving every time. Even now she knows me, and turns her head and lows gently at me when I go up to her, poor beast.

Shelled again last night, but all went over our heads or to the left. No casualties. A fatigue party in " X " line had three casualties, none severe. Early this morning a shell pitched on a small cottage about 50 yards from camp and set it on fire. It looked very picturesque in the dull grey dawn, and somehow lonely, too, for no one dared go near it, and it just burnt itself out unaided.

Rode into Divisional Headquarters after tea. It was a lovely evening, and the ride through the rich cornfields ablaze with poppies was really beautiful. As we passed the cross roads there were four horses lying by the roadside. A shell had hit them a few minutes before I arrived ; and there they lay, their poor feet thrown out awkwardly and their lips curled back to show their grey-green teeth in their death agony. My own horse went past them with his head sideways and his ears working like semaphores—it's curious how they hate the sight of their own dead. It quite spoiled the ride for me ; and every time I see a group of splendid beasts standing patiently by a dump or pulling happily at a waggon,

I cannot but think of those poor stark ugly things lying half in and half out of the golden cornfield, bathed in the peaceful sunset, with the blood-splashed dusty road churned and scarred by their lashing feet. I rode on down through the forest, the path looking beautiful, dappled with sunlight through the trees, and every now and again passing through little clouds of dancing flies, while in the ditches sometimes an early frog would croak. As we came out into the open again a Boche plane brought down an observation balloon in flames, and was himself shot down within a minute by one of our own planes, which seemed to appear from nowhere. There was a group of five balloons close together and it was quaint to see the observers from all of them leave by parachute as one man, while the balloons themselves were hauled down like things in a child's toy theatre.

I got back to camp about eight o'clock and changed for dinner. Afterwards shelling grew very intense and there was some question as to taking to the " slits." Only one or two came really into us, however, and casualties were few and slight. They were putting over incendiary shells most of the time, which look perfectly beautiful when they burst, bathing the whole area in a rich blood-red light, in which the writhing smoke and dust look like a sort of superhuman Loie Fuller in some of her most exotic creations. The Boche had his searchlights going, too, and evidently expected trouble of some sort, while our guns kept up a continuous roar from all around us. This naval gun behind us is really horrible. He has the most ear-splitting bark imaginable, and shakes your hut like a matchbox every time he fires. One gets one's sleep in between his efforts, and it is curious how one is roused by the crashing roar of his discharge, and falls asleep again so soon afterwards that one can only remember him confusedly in the morning.

Had another poorish night, mainly shelling the next field after some batteries, but we had some casualties as well. Two men were blown over by a shell and had to go down the line.

Had a quiet morning. Went after lunch with the Colonel to see the Brigadier. Had a very pleasant ride, a lovely day and a gentle breeze blowing. Dined at No. 4 Coy.

Got back to H.Q. about ten, and we were just sitting having a drink, and preparing to go to bed, when the Boche started putting gas shells over. It was an ideal night for the purpose, not a breath of wind, and the " alert " was immediately given. There were several hectic seconds while we got into our masks, and then a long period of inaction while we sat like conspirators, or members of the Inquisition, and looked at each other. After a while we took them off and found the air fairly clear, and then —— came in and told us the village was like a London fog with gas. He had gone up with a fatigue party and the Boche had put gas shells all round them. One or two of his men had had to go down, and he himself was looking as rotten as he very well could do. A three-mile walk in a respirator, however, would make anyone look, and feel, pretty seedy, so no doubt a good deal was due to that. We finally cleared off to bed and slept, or rather lay, in our masks. It was quite impossible to sleep—there is something underhand and stealthy about gas which distinguishes it from the more manly shell. You feel it may creep in furtively under your door and choke you in your sleep. Altogether a very unpleasant night.

A lovely morning ; it had rained during the very early hours, and the air was wonderfully fresh and cool. Went in the afternoon to see a six-inch Howitzer about 200 yards off, and found the Major had been at the Varsity with me. Had a very interesting hour or two there watching them firing, the shells being quite clearly visible travelling through the air.

I heard to-day that the Boche is apparently using some new type of shell containing mustard oil, which produces terrible inflammation of the skin and mucous membranes. In the afternoon we were shelled pretty vigorously, and had several casualties. A piece of about half a pound weight swished into the ground just at my feet, and the air was full of noises like big flying beetles, such as one meets in quiet summer lanes at home. The ——s had two officers killed and one wounded last night by a direct hit on a dug-out, and they have already lost three company sergeant-majors. Things seem to be pretty brisk in the line just now.

Last night the sky was the most wonderfully beautiful thing I have ever conceived. There was an enormous amount of gunning going on all around us, and the sky was heavy with black and very low-lying clouds. There was no moon, and every gun flash was thrown on to the clouds like a limelight in a theatre. The whole vault of the sky was ablaze with transient waves of fire—orange, red, yellow and violet—following so close after each other as to be almost continuous. All along the front "Very lights" danced too, some white, some red, some blue, while from time to time a "golden rain" would bathe the whole area near it in a perfect rose-pink colour. The trees stood out jet black against the flaming sky, and the whole scene was one of simply appalling beauty.

This morning was quiet, though shells came around us all the time and we had several casualties. One shell dropped about twenty yards from No. 2 bivouac, and nearly wiped half the company out.

I ought to have gone into the A.D.M.S. again to-day, but as we were having casualties I had to stay. At this very moment we are being shelled by a big naval gun, which is undoubtedly looking for the naval gun behind us.

We were sitting round quietly after dinner, and I had just written the words "behind us," above, when there came the well-known scream overhead; but this time its note was perilously clear and loud. There was a final scream, seemingly right in our ears, a deafening, crashing roar, and then a steady thudding rain of earth and stones on the mess roof and windows. On going out to inspect, we found it had dropped just outside the hut in which the second in command and I live, the edge of the crater being exactly twelve feet from the foot of my bed and his. The hole is an enormous one; certainly a naval gun did it; and it gives one a very quaint feeling to think of the " might have been." There is nothing to do, however; so having finished this diary I shall turn in to bed and try to sleep. I wonder what to-morrow, or rather to-night, may have in store for me.

Had a very unpleasant night, shelled a good deal, and was about most of the time. The noise from our own guns is by now so terrific that it is really quite impossible to get any sleep unless you are dead tired, and then only for a few minutes. My servant dug up the nose cap of the shell out of the crater last night, and I shall keep it as a souvenir.

Went into the A.D.M.S. this morning and had a charming ride there and back. Went up the line with the C.O. in the afternoon, and found things enormously changed even since I was there last. There has been very heavy shelling all round the château; and the new track, only built a day or two ago and intended for use when we go in for the big push, is already bordered along its entire length by shell holes. Some spy no doubt. There was a good deal of stuff going over both ways, but nothing very near us, and we turned into the headquarters of the battalion in reserve. Found their C.O. talking to two other officers, both old friends of his, from another battalion in the line. We stayed and talked for a while and then his two friends went on, one of them looking very smart in his white buckskin breeches and swinging a little fly-whisk in his hand. We ourselves left a few minutes later, and had gone about fifty yards along the trench when the C.O. sent me back with a message, saying he would wait for me at the corner. I was gone about five minutes, and we then hurried on to catch up the two others. Almost immediately a runner came down the trench towards us and said, " There's one officer killed and one wounded just along here, sir."

We hurried along the trench, all bright with silver grass and poppies, and came on

128

poor —— lying on the yellow mud-stained duckboards, with his silk shirt ripped off to show his fair skin, and a dark red hole in his right side. His fly-whisk was still in his hand.

He was obviously dying fast, and was already leaden coloured and cold. I clapped a field dressing over his wound, but he had bled all round in a sticky lake already, and I turned him over and fastened him to the stretcher which the runner had got. He groaned once or twice and then said : " I can't breathe. I think I must be dying," and so his last words were his truest. He was dead before we got him five yards along the trench. His companion had the whole of his chest blown in and must have died instantly. It was a horrible business, having seen them laughing and happy not ten minutes before. The curious thing is that it was only my going back on the message that prevented the C.O. and myself from having joined the party, in which case we should all four most probably have been done in. As we were carrying him back we met his friend the other C.O., who had just heard he had been hit. He came up to us. " Is —— hit badly ? " he asked. I said, " Very badly, I'm afraid." " Do you think he'll be all right ? " " I'm afraid he's dead now," I replied. He turned round in the trench so that his back was towards us, threw his trench stick down with a gesture like an angry child, and said, "The swine ! " quite low and quietly to himself. Then he stood back in a traverse while we went on past him. We saw a number of wounded and dead being carried along as we went home, and shelling was pretty bad all the way back. The mess was rather depressed in the evening, for they were both very good fellows and very popular. To-morrow night we go into the line ourselves.

There was a good deal of shelling all last night, and several casualties. Had very

little sleep at all. This morning went to
——'s funeral in the afternoon with the
C.O., and a most impressive thing it was.
While we were standing round the grave
there was a fight going on between a Boche
plane and one of ours just over us. One
couldn't look up, of course, but one could
hear their machine-guns going all the
time.

Got back to the farm about five, and we
were shelled steadily all the evening and
had many casualties. While we were
standing by waiting to march into the line,
a shell hit one of the cookers about thirty
yards off with a noise of a million iron-
mongers' shops dropped simultaneously
from heaven. It killed all four horses.

We moved off at ten o'clock for the front
line. A lovely still night, with a low-lying
mist and a hot heavy smell in the air.
Owing to the shelling we kept 200 yards
between Coys., and I marched last with
my bearers. They are always a wonderful
thing to me, these reliefs at night. The

absence of all human friendliness that permeates every thing— the men talking in hoarse whispers, with now and again a flash of a match as a cigarette is lit—the steady tramp, tramp of the feet and the jingle of kit—and over all the roar of the guns and the rattling crash of bursting shells—a really unforgettable experience. We swung along towards the village, and then turned left across the main road, which was being, as usual, heavily shelled. Once or twice we had to halt for troops coming out, and once or twice while dead horses or men were being dragged either from the road or from the trench. Once, when we halted because a shell had just dropped across the trench and blown a great crater in it, the moon came from behind some misty clouds and showed everything like a scene in a ballet. There was a gun just to my right shoulder; and every time she went off I was deafened, till I put my finger to my ear to stop it.

The trench was passing under some

beautiful willows at the time, and the sides of it were all sparkling in dewy grasses and flowers, while the duckboards stood out under my feet as if phosphorescent. I thought how lovely to smell the dampness of the grasses and to put my hand to the elbow in them—and they smelt of sulphur and shell gas only. It was wonderful to see how vividly some things stood out in the moonlight and mist. The trenches are shored up with split logs, and a great deal of silver birch is used for this purpose. The effect of these is like big silver splashes on a black velvet background, and the play of light and shadow on them as the men go past is simply entrancing. We had a few casualties going in, but got to our line all right. No. 4 Coy. was to stay in the reserve line, and I had to push on up to the front line alone, since the M.O. was not being relieved " in reserve " till the night after.

There was a good deal of shelling all the way up to the front line, and a lot of machine-gun firing too. This I detest, for the trenches, as I know too well from daylight walks, are too shallow to give any protection to the head unless you stoop double, and it was very unpleasant indeed to hear machine-guns rattling away, and an occasional " pfing " of a bullet go over and across the trench.

Got up to the front line about midnight, and took over from the ——s. The aid post is still in very good order, except in one place, where it has had two direct hits from 5.9's and the roof has caved in a bit.

One of our working parties last night came unexpectedly upon one of the enemy forward posts. The leading man of our party, an Irish navvy in private life, lifted his head with infinite caution and peered into the black hole of the trench, where he saw an unsuspecting Boche leaning on his rifle and dozing gently. Withdrawing his head as cautiously as before, the Irishman leaned down towards his mate and said, in a tense whisper : " For the love of Mercy, lend us your shovel." His whole frame a-quiver with expectancy, shovel in hand, he again raised himself, hung poised for a second like a veritable shadow of death over the dreamy Boche, and then, with one terrific blow, almost severed his head from his shoulders. "It's a fine tool, is a shovel," said he, and returned it, one feels almost reluctantly, to its owner. That pleases me, the cobbler returning instinctively to his last !

Had a poorish night. Up all the time with front line casualties, and some pretty bad cases, too. Several died after on the way down to me or in the aid post, and the little open space in front was soon full of stretchers with stiff khaki figures on them. We were heavily shelled all night, and had to wear our respirators for about two hours because of gas shells. I have had practically no sleep for four days, and am pretty well dead beat. The aid post and my dugout are in a side trench running parallel to the Boche line, and the front parapet of the trench is just about at ground level, so the journey from my dug-out to the aid post doesn't take me more than a few seconds, in consequence.

Had a quiet morning. Very little shelling from the Boche and only the steady swish and flutter to be heard of our shells going over. The air was full of planes, and now and again they would put up a scrap or two; but one is too used to that even to look. This château where my aid post is must have a been a lovely place in pre-war days, and is now used as Battalion Headquarters. The cellars are fairly good and have been pretty well sandbagged ; but I shouldn't like a direct hit on the mess, it would go through like paper. There was a practice barrage on our front at 3.30 and 5.50, so one could do nothing but sit in one's dug-out and wait for the noise to stop. Sleep was impossible, since we have a battery just behind the aid post near the lake, and the bark comes down the dug-out tunnel like a megaphone. To-night I go down to " reserve " to relieve the M.O. there; so let's hope it's quieter.

Later.

This is written from the Base Hospital, where I am now. I left the front line on the night of the 22nd, about ten o'clock, having spent the two preceding hours in my respirator. The Boche was putting large numbers of gas shells over, and the air was very thick. The second in command had been up the line and was going back to "reserve," so we returned together, leaving my servant and bearer-Sergeant to bring my kit and instruments along. It was very thick going down the communication trench, and the air was full of gas, so we had to keep the mask over our

mouths and hold our noses with both
hands, since one could not see with the
goggles up. The trench was blown in in
a great many places, and the Boche had
evidently got it taped, for he was bursting
5.9's and pip-squeaks with the most extraordinary accuracy right along it. We
hurried along as fast as possible, though
the respirators made it slow going, the
runner first and myself last, when there
was a shrill scream, an echoing " raang,"
and I felt something like a thunderbolt hit
me on the top of the head and neck. It
threw me off my feet about five yards
along the trench, and I came with my knee
an awful welt on the edge of a broken
duckboard or something. The pain of my
knee kept me from losing consciousness,
that and the clear-cut knowledge that if I
lost consciousness there I should lose it for
good, so I got up on my feet again by holding on to the wire shoring up the trench.
My companion had heard the burst and
me fall, and turned round and shouted :

138

"Are you all right, Doc ? " I knew if I said I was hit he'd come back and insist on doing something, he being a terribly fidgetty old fellow, in which case the next shell would probably bag us both, so I said, " Yes, I'm all right," and started off down the trench again. I got about ten yards when I felt something hot running down my neck and back, and putting my hand up I found I was bleeding like a pig from my head. Then I began to be unable to see properly and couldn't keep steady on the duckboards, while getting round places where the trench was blown in was literally hell. I stumbled once or twice more, and finally found I couldn't keep up, so I had to shout to the others not to go so fast as I had been hit. My friend came back, took my pack off me, and put me between himself and the runner, since I could walk all right if they didn't go too fast, and we started on again. It seemed a thousand miles from " reserve ; " and when men coming up the line blundered into me and

knocked me up against the trench side, I
could have struck them; but I managed
to go almost all the way, and then couldn't
carry on any longer. I " came to " in the
aid post, with a Gunner M.O. dressing my
head. My friend was for sending me down
at once, as was the M.O.; but I thought if
I had a quiet night I should be all right
to carry on next morning, so we compro-
mised, and I went to his dug-out and lay
down, while the Gunner M.O. carried on
for me till morning. In the morning I felt
a bit worse and doubted myself whether
I could carry on. We had had to wear our
respirators again for most of the night,
and I had vomited a lot as well, so I knew
I was pretty badly concussed, and what
with one thing and another I felt pretty
rotten. I had to go down, in any case, to
the Advanced Dressing Station, to get my
Anti-Tetanic Serum, and when I went
there the M.O. wouldn't let me go back.

He put me in an ambulance and shot me
straight down to the Corps Main Dressing

Station, from whence I was shot down to a Casualty Clearing Station.

My A.D.M.S. very kindly came in next morning and talked things over with me, insisted on my going down, and promised he would see that I got back to the Battalion again as soon as I was ready, so I had to make up my mind to it. Before leaving the aid post, I had told my servant not to unpack my things, but to get on to my bed and lie down himself, for he was completely done up ; so when I got to the C.C.S., and knew I was going down the line, I had to wire our adjutant to send him to me with my kit. Instead of him, however, another fellow brought it, and told me that about two hours after I left they put a 5.9 clean through the roof, and the entire aid post went up, including my poor fellow. I'm very cut-up about him; he was a splendid lad and a most devoted servant.

The one that hit me apparently burst close overhead and completely caved in my helmet, making a fairly nasty cut in my scalp and pushing me forward with the concussion. If it hadn't been for my helmet it would surely have pushed my skull in like a tomato. As it was, it just missed breaking my neck. On the whole, I got off very lightly.

After lunch to-day I went for my first walk up the hill for some fresh air, and coming past the cemetery I saw there was an officer's funeral on. It's a very simple affair and yet awfully impressive. I had never seen a real one before. The coffin was wheeled up to the churchyard on a little hand-bier covered with the Union Jack, and behind it were marching a firing squad of about twenty men. When they got near the grave the coffin was carried down and the soldiers formed up by the graveside while the service was read. There were two of the boy's people there, an elderly lady and a younger girl, and they stood almost alone in a little space on the other side of the grave. While the parson

142

drones away at the service, the men stand
with their rifles with the tip of the barrel
on their foot and their hands crossed on
the butt, and the Lieutenant, quite a young
lad, stands also to attention with his cane
by his leg, looking very self-conscious and
trying not to see the relatives, at whom he
is staring directly, across a narrow strip of
trench. It made a very impressive picture
under the bright sun. On one side of the
churchyard were the usual French tombs,
with all sorts of fantastic wirework ornaments and flowers in little glass cases like
greenhouses, and on the other the larger
newer part reserved for soldiers, with plain
white wooden crosses with a number on,
packed as close as the men can lie, and just
plain grass on top. A big, loose-limbed
Canadian in a slouch hat was loafing
among the French graves, looking curiously at the ornaments, and across the low
red-topped wall some old women and boys
were turning the hay in the next field. I
was near enough to see the faces of the

firing party, staring down at the ground with their brown hands on the rifle butts, some so short that they could rest their chins on the backs of their hands, and some big, lanky lads whose heads were a foot above. The sergeant in charge was a typical " regular," with a square hard, expressionless face and a thick red, hairy neck ; and his clothes, his hyper-polished belt and leathers, and the whole set of his self-confident, earnest, stupid head on his magnificent shoulders, was enough to epitomize the hopeless waste and uselessness of the whole system to which he belongs. Suddenly there was a sharp word of command, " Squad, fix bayonets " ; a small man from the end of the row runs two steps forward, halts, and with incredible mechanical precision drops his rifle between his knees, whips his bayonet out, snaps it in place to the accompaniment of nineteen other snaps, takes two brisk steps back, and it is done. As one man the whole line is once more rigid and expressionless.

Another bark, and they present arms, with
a pretty flash of sun on the bright steel,
and then, ever so clear and sharp, sounds a
bugle from the rear. It is the last post.
It is a quaint, pathetic little call, and it is
just too much for the younger girl, who
breaks down completely long before the
last broken little note has ended. The
older lady puts her hand inside her arm.
Almost before on can realise it, there is a
hoarse, thin bark from the Lieutenant, a
series of stamps and noises of boots and
harness, and the firing party has formed
up and is swinging past one out of the gate,
the Sergeant bringing up the rear file, with
his habitual fierce look and his sharply
turned-up waxed moustache. One feels
that, if he has any thought at all in his
devoted head, it is doubtless a sense of
bitter hatred against the rear-rank man,
who was, it is just possible, a fraction of a
second late with his snap in " fixing bayonets." Otherwise, it's a fine day, he has
had a little pleasant exercise combined

L

with duty, and his uniform and kit do become him remarkably. The two ladies come along talking to the clergyman, a youngish man whose collar looks too big for him, and who excuses himself at the gate as he has "nine other services to conduct before the Presbyterian Minister begins his." The two ladies shake hands with him, the elder quite firmly and gracefully, holding her little green satchel and umbrella delicately by the other hand; and then, with tears running quietly over her face, she gives her arm to the younger girl, and they walk down the winding hill together, back into the village alone.

Came over to France again after my sick leave, and had two days at the Base. Went up the line by passenger train, with the help of ——, the R.T.O., and had a very easy journey as far as Poperinghe, finishing by lorry. I heard that the Battalion was in camp on the Elverdinghe-Woestan

main road, so went straight there, as it was
nearer than the A.D.M.S. and I wanted to
make sure of getting back to them. It is
really very pleasant to be with them again.
The camp had been badly bombed the
night before, and the M.O. whom I relieved
told me he had been up all night while
bombs were being dropped in camp.

I had a long talk with the C.O. after
dinner, and he told me what a magnificent
show the Battalion had made in the
" push " I missed, when they took all their
objectives.

An N.C.O. told me, too, how, when the
Battalion was advancing at their slow
march across the open under an appalling
machine-gun and rifle fire, and when shells
were falling all round and amongst them
and casualties were at their heaviest, he
saw a hare get up and run along the line,
and man after man took a pot shot at her
as she ran, and laughed and joked amongst
themselves when they missed her. The
C.O. tells me that my locum did splendidly

all day, for we had a good many casualties, and the shell that got him was a most unlucky one. He had his aid post in a shell hole, and came to the C.O. to ask if he could go back and try and find more cover, as he did not think it was safe to stay where he was. The C.O. gave his permission, and he saw him go back with his orderly. A few minutes later a private came in and said he had seen a shell drop right at his feet, and he and his orderly were literally blown to pieces. Poor old ——, he was a real nice lad.

This camp where we are is a good one as regards position, but too near the railway and road, and we are therefore shelled all day, and bombed all night, and casualties occur all the time. We move into the the line in a day or two, however, so it does not really matter.

Had a most interesting trip up the line to-day, gong as far as advanced Battalion

Headquarters, and seeing all the new ground we have taken. It gives one quite a thrill to go up to the point where our old front line was, and where one has spent so many unpleasant hours, and then to go on still further and walk on ground which one's own Battalion has just taken. It's true that I myself had no hand in the taking of it, unfortunately, but still one was for some time part of the Battalion when the preparations were going on; and it is a splendid thing to stand now on the ridge and look over the sunlit stretch of country we have taken, and see the fringe of trees that marks our next objective. It's very unpleasant in the line now, for there is, of course, no cover but slits, and the Boche shells night and day to hold up the advance. He put over 7,000 gas shells last night on our front.

Got back to Battalion Headquarters for lunch, and lectured on first aid in the afternoon and evening.

We were very badly shelled last night in camp, and I was up almost all night. I find I can't stand shelling like I could; the noise seems to go into my head and echo there, and I have to hold myself down with both hands so as not to jump when they are near. I suppose I shall get over it; a head wound always leaves something of the sort for a time; but it certainly is very unpleasant. It is all the more annoying since the Battalion push has been postponed, and I would not have come out so early if I had known that.

Rode in to see the A.D.M.S., and had a charming ride back in the evening. It's wonderful how good a bit of peaceful country looks to one these days.

Another bad night, but it quieted down about 7 a.m. This afternoon we were having tea when about nine Boche planes came over, flying very low. They dropped a bomb just outside the camp, and the

C.O. ordered us into the slits. Just as we got in they dropped another bomb in the camp, and I saw bits of canvas and wood go up like a rocket. I knew it had got a bivouac, so I ran across and saw quite the ugliest sight I have yet seen out here. The bomb had dropped clean inside the pit where five men were lying, and one man had been simply blown to ribbons, and was literally dripping from the pit-sides. One man had both feet blown off, another had one blown off, and another had his head very badly wounded. While I was getting them out, with an N.C.O. from the next slit, two more bombs dropped about twenty and forty yards off, but did no damage. Then they dropped another about ten yards off, and you could hear the stuff going past you like bees. It missed me and the N.C.O. and killed an A.S.C. man, through the door of a dug-out just next to us, and also wounded one of our officers who was lying down in the mess.

Then they flew on, and we could hear

them dropping bombs in the camps near us. It was an awful job getting our fellows on to stretchers. One knew them all so well, and under a bright sun it looked too horrible. The poor lad with his two feet off was quite conscious, and obviously dying. I patched him up and got him on a stretcher, gave him a cigarette and left him, when he called me back. He said something which I couldn't catch, for his lips and face were very cut about and bleeding ; so I wiped his mouth, and he said quite clearly and quietly, " Shall I live, sir ? " " Live," I said, " Good Lord, yes—you'll be as right as rain when you're properly dressed and looked after." " Thank you, sir," he said, and went on smoking his cigarette. He died as they were getting him on the ambulance.

I had just finished them off, and had gone to my tent to wash, when a man came from a Divisional Ammunition camp next to ours to say that they had a lot of casualties and no M.O. ; so I had to go

across and patch them up. They had about
ten killed and a lot of wounded, and I was
about an hour and a half there. They had
had one bomb clean in their horse lines,
too, and lost 34 horses. It was perfectly
ghastly to see them, some standing round
snuffling at their dead mates, while others
just stood and fidgetted, with bright little
streams of blood spurting from their soft
sleek bodies. I was very glad to get away.

We were shelled very badly after dinner,
and I had a good deal to do. Altogether a
poor day.

We moved to Rugby Camp to-day,
further up the line; and a very unhealthy
spot it is. The ——s were shelled out of
it last night, and I should say we shall be
to-night. They had got twelve six-inch
naval shells into it before we'd got our
tents pitched.

I feel very depressed to-night for some
reason. I haven't had much sleep lately,

and I have had a shocking head for several days, too, so perhaps that's it. We go into the line in three days, and when we come out the whole Division is to be taken out to rest, so if I can stick this next few days, I shall be all right.

Had a real bad night, shelling continually all round the camp. In addition, it rained hard and blew a devil of a gale, which made my job very unpleasant. We had a good few casualties, and had two cookers blown to blazes; but the C.O. thought it best to stay where we were as shelling was so bad everywhere. All this morning and afternoon they have been putting eight-inch stuff into a battery just short of us, but fortunately nothing has come into us. The noise, however, is appalling, and that worries me as much as anything these days.

Had to attend a Court Martial to-day

on one of our men who had deserted before the last push and had just been captured behind the lines. He is a pitiful degenerate, has drunk a lot in his time, and is obviously of no use to anyone. I had to inspect him last night to say if he was fit for his trial, and he told me all his history. This morning, to my amazement, he asked to have me at his trial to speak for him, though I had given him no encouragement last night, when he cried and behaved like a perfect beast all the time. I went to the trial determined to give him no help of any sort, for I detest his type; and seeing so many good fellows go out during the night's shelling made me all the more bitter against him for trying to back down. I really hoped he would be shot, as indeed was anticipated by all of us.

However, when I was called, he stood so drearily between his two big sentries, looking so hopelessly forlorn and lonely, with his dirty face and white cheeks, that before I knew what I was doing I found myself

trying to let him down gently. All the
time I was talking he kept his eyes on me,
and I really never saw such a look of pitiful
appeal as he managed to get into them,
while he kept wetting his lips and swallow-
ing, and wiping the sweat from his dirty
brown forehead. I said I knew he had
always been a man of a highly nervous
temperament whose self-control was practically nil, and that I considered he was
much below the standard of the ordinary
man in every way mentally. Whether I
did it or not, I don't know, but he got off,
and came creeping round to my aid post
afterwards to thank me. I talked pretty
straight to him then, for I felt as I had felt
before I saw him cowering between the
two guards, and told him he had damned
well got to pull himself together and make
a fresh start. He promised he would, and
asked if he might come and talk to me
sometimes, for the other men in his
company didn't understand and would
scarcely speak to him. Of course, I said

he could; but it will be an infernal nuisance, and in any case he'll never make
anything, and will probably bolt again the
first chance he gets. They tell me he'll
probably get shot by his own mates the
next time we go over the top, so it's a
bright look-out anyway, poor devil!

We are under orders to move at one
hour's notice. It's an awful bore, because
one cannot leave the camp at all; and it
gets very monotonous sitting round day
after day, being shelled and gassed and
doing nothing. It's really worse than being
in the line.

Had a splendid night. Hardly any
shelling, except a few gas shells early on,
and I slept from 10.30 till 4.30—the best
night I've had since I came out. A fine
rain was falling when I got up at 7.15, and
I had a rather dismal bath in the open in
consequence, but it cleared up about ten,
and has been a glorious day ever since.

Have drifted around camp, looked at a
12-in. howitzer just near us, helped men to
fill sandbags for our new mess, and generally done nothing. Now there is a perfectly wonderful sunset, with exquisitely
pretty little fleecy clouds strewn over a
sky of a wonderful lemon yellow—I should
like very much to see it over the heather
on Cobham Common on my way out to
the Hautboy in the old Rolls.

Another fairly good night till 4 a.m.,
when the Boche put down a terrific amount
of stuff all over and around us, and I was
pretty busy in consequence. At six o'clock
a wire came from Brigade to say we must
be ready to start at five minutes' notice,
so at once the camp was like a beehive.
There were all sorts of rumours going
round. Some said the Boche had broken
through and was over the canal, others
that the Division in the line on our left
had taken a bad knock, and we had to go

there and take over, and all were tremend-
ously excited. It was a perfect treat to see
how keen the men were when there was a
prospect of a scrap; and I must say, it was
really a relief to think we should be giving
a bit back of what we had had so plenti-
fully handed us this last few days. However, time passed and nothing happened,
and later in the day we heard that the
Boche had got the idea we were making a
push, and had put down a pretty stiff
barrage on the front line. The Battalion
holding it had got the wind up and asked
for reinforcements, thinking the Boche
himself was going to attack. Altogether a
pretty quaint affair.

I hear this morning that my deserter
friend was absent on parade this morning;
and as we go into the line to-morrow the
inference is obvious. Poor, stupid, im-
potent creature, caught in a machine as
useless as himself—he's done for now,
without a hope.

Went for a walk round Boesinghe Château after lunch, and looked at my former aid post. It had received a direct hit from an eight-inch since I left it, and has just gone up like a heap of bricks. The trench is all blown in, too, and on the whole I'm glad I wasn't in it at the time.

Later.

This is written in No. 46 Casualty Clearing Station, Proven.

We left camp on the night of the 17th, about 7.30, my party having thirty men extra, who were to do nightly patrol work and to live at the aid post at Ruisseau Farm with my bearers. We had a quiet relief as far as White Hope Corner, where there was a lot of shelling but no casualties. In Boesinghe High Street, shelling was very intense and, of course, the guide for our party had cleared off and couldn't be found. Finally, the Adjutant of the Battalion we were reliving had to come himself and show us the way.

We got going a few minutes afterwards, and were very glad to get away, for they were all over the High Street with 5.9's and big stuff, and we were too crowded to be pleasant. We had no trouble until we got about half a mile over the canal, and then we saw they were shelling the duck-boards ahead of us. One burst clean on the boards about fifty yards ahead of us, and one knew it would be a very near thing if we got the party past it before another from that same gun came along. No time was lost, anyhow, our officer and the Adjutant setting the pace like greyhounds in front, and the party streaking after them in single file as hard as they could walk. In a few seconds along she came, obviously very near; there was a final crescendo shriek, and a tremendous flash and " raang," just off the boards on the left of the tail of the party. I felt something catch me an awful welt under the ear, and saw a perfect constellation for a second, and went down on my knees for a rest !

M

Then I heard the man next me say, " I think he's dead, sir," and I found I was practically kneeling on the man marching ahead of me. He had his head twisted under him, and his arms and legs all tangled in his kit, and I thought he was dead, too. The quaint thing was that my neighbour thought I'd knelt down to look at the other fellow, and had no idea I was hit. The rest of the party had not missed us, but had streaked on into the dark, leaving only Padre, my Corporal, and two other soldiers, who were friends of the man who was hit and had seen him fall. I pushed my hand inside his shirt but could feel nothing, and had just made up my mind he was dead and was wondering if I could walk myself, when he suddenly gave the queerest sort of gurgling cry, just as though he knew we were leaving him. Then I knew he was living still, and we had to get him somehow to the aid post; though how, I couldn't imagine, for I felt every minute as though I were going off myself. We were a devil of a time getting him on the stretcher. My Corporal had been helping me to get his kit off, and our hands were so covered with blood that we couldn't unfasten the stretcher strap, and finally had to cut it. They put a good deal of stuff all round us before we got moving, and I was quite glad to get away from the spot. I put his two pals on to carrying him first, for I really couldn't have carried him an inch just then, and wanted the Corporal to carry with me, because he's trained to it and would keep me on the duckboards.

It seemed a million miles to the aid post, instead of about two miles, and every time I knelt down to get the straps over my shoulders for my turn I could scarcely keep my head off the duckboards. To make matters worse, I knew we ought to pass near the Advanced Dressing Station, but I was so muzzy-headed I couldn't remember where it was, and none of the others knew either. We made one try up a by-track and couldn't find it, and as I knew I couldn't go much further I thought it best to head straight for the aid post. We finally got there somehow, and having put him down on the trestles, the Corporal turned round and said, " Why, you're wounded, sir ! " " Yes," I said, " go and ask Captain —— to carry on for a bit." So saying I sat down on a biscuit box, and was horribly sick on some unfortunate patients lying in the aid post for collection.

The M.O. came along and would hear no reason whatever. I explained that I was done up then simply with carrying that infernal stretcher, and that I should be perfectly fit next morning. Every time I started to say something he burst out in his broadest Scotch, " Ye're going down. I tell ye ye're going down." Finally, being in no mood to stand his accent, I went down. I was carried down, for I really couldn't have walked a yard, and spent the night at the A.D.S. I couldn't sleep much, but next morning I really felt less tired, so

I persuaded the M.O. there to let me go back, and got up to the aid post about 8.30 a.m., when things were fairly quiet. I relieved my Scotch friend, sent a note across to the C.O. to say I was back, received a characteristic reply congratulating me on my " self-inflicted wound," and then thought all was well.

Just after lunch, however, another M.O. came up from the Field Ambulance with a note from their Colonel, ordering me to report " wounded " to him immediately. It was very disappointing, for I very much wanted to see the push on our right, but down I had to go. I came down here quietly and have been here ever since, nursing a chewed-up ear and a thick head, but otherwise very well. The A.D.M.S. has promised he will not send me down if I stay here till the Battalion comes out of the line, and that I may rejoin them there, so I just lie here all day and eat and read and sleep.

Plenty of casualties coming through,

but the news is good and all our objectives
are being taken, so all is well.

There is one lad here from Scarborough,
he admits he is only sixteen, who has a
badly smashed knee and may have to have
it amputated. He generally screams the
place down when it is dressed, being
a poor wizened, red-headed little coward
at the best of times. But I have sat and
held his hand this last three days while he
is being dressed, threatened to hit him in
the stomach every time he shouts, told him
he's no Yorkshireman and, as a Lancashire man myself, I'm ashamed of him,
till now he goes through it like a little
brick, with the tears running down his face
all the time. As soon as he sees it's his
turn he shouts out to me, if I'm in the
ward : " Doctor, come 'ere," in his broad
Yorkshire, snatches at my hand like a
child, and hangs on to it all the time. I
generally put a piece of cotton wool over
his eyes (we call that " pullin' the curtain
down," he and I) but the sight of the hole

in his leg with the tubes sticking out of it really scares him more than the pain, and he's just getting now to be able to stand the wool off his face while they put him back into his splint.

" Ye can pull th' curtain oop," I'll hear a muffled voice say, and when I do, there he is with his poor little adenoid face all puffed up with crying, and looking like a scared child with his brick-red hair and bright-coloured cheeks and lips. He's getting better every day; but how he mustered courage to join the army beats me. I asked him if he was scared in the trenches, and he said " No, but I was a bit skeered when we 'ad to get o'er th' top ! "

Came back to the Battalion, and am very glad to get here. We're in Penton Camp at present, not a bad place, but too near the railway to be safe from planes.

Had a very good champagne dinner and slept like a top all night.

A few bombs were dropped in a field next the camp this morning, but none in our camp. Went for a ride this afternoon and came back about 4.30. On my way I passed a by-road with a notice reading "No Tanks or Caterpillars this way." What a world we live in when such a notice excites no comment.

Had a charming ride in the quaint fields and villages round here and came home to tea. After tea I did a bit of putting the weight, and had a very close match with Drill-Sergeant Copping. He beat me by about a foot, but I feel still a bit feeble after my knock, and believe I can beat him when I am stronger again. Took him on at sandbag throwing afterwards and wore him down at that all right. The C.O. joined in—and we had a very pleasant hour before dinner. The latter has just come back from leave and brought a brace of grouse, so some of my champagne will go very well with them over dinner.

Heard a very quaint thing to-day. One

man in this new draft is, in peace time, a very well-to-do stockbroker, who has kept out of the army till the last moment. He was being put through his paces by the Sergeant-Major, together with the rest of his squad, and was not moving nearly smartly enough. After several pretty candid remarks from the Sergeant-Major, the latter finally burst out, " Put some work into it, man, put some work into it ! Anyone would think you'd never done any work in your life ! " At this the recruit, goaded beyond all endurance, retorted plaintively, " Well, to tell you the truth, sir, I really never have ! " and then, realising the enormity of his offence, said, "I beg your pardon, sir," and went on silently sweating blood for no purpose.

Had a poor night. Bombed all to hell for about two hours, and was up most of the night. It's really very annoying that I can't stand noise better, for apart from that I am really very fit.

A few bombs were dropped in a field next the camp this morning, but none in our camp. Went for a ride in the afternoon, and came back about 4.30. As I passed out of the camp I saw my deserter's face looking over the top of a cowhouse half-door, the cowhouse being the guard-room. He has evidently been caught again, and is a dead certainty to be shot this time. It was rather horrible, however, seeing him looking like a wild beast, cowed and caged, framed in the dark half-doorway, and staring out, all unshaven and wan, into the bright, sunlit field. One can't help hating a condition of affairs which makes cowardice a crime, and forces one already poor specimen of manhood into something too horribly near a beast. After all, cowardice ought not to be a crime, and yet one has seen so many splendid fellows lay down their lives so

bravely that one can find no pity for such
as he.

Another poor night, a good many bombs
falling near but none in the camp. We
moved in the morning to Herzeele, and
Battalion Headquarters is in a very charming place, formerly a convent. Everyone
has gone now, except the Mother Superior
and one or two of the older nuns, and very
charming ladies they are. They must
see some rather unusual and " worldly "
things from time to time, but they seem to
like to talk to us, and are always very
smiling and charming. Had a quiet morning and afternoon and went to bed early,
but for some reason slept badly.

We are giving a dinner to the Brigade
to-morrow, and two other officers and myself went to-day to the base to get fish.
Had a quiet journey in, " jumping " lorries
and experiencing to the full the insigni-

ficance of the mere infantry in the eyes of
the A.S.C., who have cars to spare and
rarely hear a shell burst. One of my com-
panions was so disgusted on one occasion
that he told the officer what he thought,
and was very nearly put under arrest by
the Colonel. Got to the Base about 4
p.m. and had a good lunch in Boulogne,
having left the Battalion at 9 a.m. Found
all shops shut and could get no fish.

We saw one of the Consultants to the
Base who, when he heard of our difficulty
getting down, offered to send us back in
his car after dinner. This was really too
good to believe, for otherwise we should
have had to start back at 6, and get no
dinner at all.

Started back about 9 p.m., after a very
good dinner, and passed through a perfect
barrage of bombs round Cassel and St.
Omer. It got so bad at one time that we
stopped the car under a house-side and got
into the ditch for a while. But it got no
better, so we decided to push on. Got

home about 11 p.m., after a very amusing day.

Heard this morning that we are to go over the top again next Sunday, or thereabouts, and must expect heavy casualties, as the job we have to do is a pretty unpleasant one. So that's that! The dinner has been postponed a night.

Went to Dunkirk to buy fish, and found it badly knocked about with bombs.

Had a very amusing day, and got back about 7 p.m. Had a quiet but very good dinner, and went off to bed early.

I had the best night I have had for some time, and slept till I was called. Had a practice attack in the morning, and in the afternoon I went to bed and lay down for an hour or two. Had a football match, at five o'clock, against the officers of the

——s ; and some Boche planes livened things up a bit by dropping bombs all round us most of the time. None came in our field, however, and we hadn't even to stop playing. Had our postponed dinner in the evening, and a very excellent one it turned out to be. Afterwards we adjourned to a marquee in the field, and only just in time, for some thirty of the younger fellows were well illuminated by this time, and would infallibly have reduced everything to atoms. We had wrestling, cock-fighting and general ragging, the marquee was let down upon a medley of men, chairs, and flaming paraffin lamps, various people injured various parts of their persons more or less acutely and, in a word, the dinner and evening was an enormous success.

They bombed us as usual, and one of the servants was hit slightly coming across from the kitchen, but nothing serious. We held the dinner in the Convent schoolroom, which is still used by the village children, and it was quite impressive to

see written in large letters on the black-
board, evidently by a woman's hand, the
inscription. "*Jusqu'au bout*" and underneath an English and French flag pinned.
There is no doubt this war is almost a
sacred thing to the French people, instead
of, as to us, merely a thoroughly boring
affair which has got some moments of
thrill to make it bearable.

A very quiet day. Did not go to bed till
very late and had to be up again at 7.15,
and everybody feeling, naturally, like
death. Had another practice in the afternoon; raining all day, very dismal. Saw a
most extraordinary letter found on a dead
Frenchman on our right flank, from his
wife. In it she said she enclosed him 100
francs, which she had earned by giving
herself to soldiers in her billet. She sent
it to him with her heart's love; for since
he could get no leave she knew he must

have some woman to love where he was. This money was to enable him to get someone clean. All she asked was that he should choose someone as like her as possible, and remember always that her heart was his, and that she prayed night and morning for his safety and quick return. No man could understand that attitude, at least no Englishman, I know.

To-morrow we move up the line again, and are due in the line Monday night. The Commanding Officer tells me he expects fairly heavy casualties; and certainly the number of pill-boxes on our front is simply appalling in the aeroplane photographs.

Had a very quiet afternoon reading indoors, as it is raining hard and blowing a gale.

A quiet night and no bombing. The stormy weather, I imagine, is too much for

them. Walked round the camp and in-
spected billets early ; and then did the
practice attack again in the morning, and
also in the afternoon. Came back, had
tea, and spent the late afternoon reading
and talking.

Went to bed early last night and slept
like a top. There was a high wind blowing and more rain, so no planes came over.
This morning broke very dull and cold,
and since the mess was cleared up early
for packing, one had nowhere to go but
wander, blue with cold, up and down the
village street.

Started for our new camp at 4.10, and
had a very dismal journey, since it blew a
devil of a cold wind and rained all the way.
Arrived in camp wet through and chilled
literally to the bone, and found we had to
wait over an hour for dinner as the mess-
kit lorry had got stuck in the mud coming

over. I am writing this in clothes which are absolutely wet through, and have the prospect of going to bed in a very damp valise as well.

Had a perfectly monstrous night, and have never been more agonisingly cold. I scarcely slept at all, the cold wind making it quite impossible, and the rain dripping through the tent, which was an old one, in many places. Had a quiet and very dreary day in camp, raining in torrents all day and a high wind blowing. Further details of the last push show that it was a real success. The weather looks like spoiling ours, however, or at any rate making it a hundred times more difficult.

Another bitterly cold night, and it has rained in sheets all day, with a full gale blowing. We moved up to Forest Area by train as far as possible—travelling in cattle trucks *" en prince ! "* We then marched, the wind being perfectly appalling, and heavy driving rain all the time. This camp is a very good one; we are in huts and very comfortable, but go into the line to-morrow evening at five. It's not very pleasant, listening to the rain driving against the mess and the howling of the wind outside, and to know that to-morrow night we shall spend lying out entirely unprotected in shell holes till Zero hour. A wait from eight at night till four next morning does not attract one in the least under such conditions, especially as our last meal will be at six at night, and we shall have nothing but chocolate, etc., till the final objective is reached. This last meal will be a queer affair, I imagine, since one knows that some of us will certainly not come out again. However, one can just do one's job and hope for the best. Have written to-day to ——, ——, and mother. I hope they will not have to be posted.

Later.

The day before the push was another day of rain and wind, and all morning and afternoon was spent getting ready to go into the line.

We left camp at 4 p.m., in heavy rain, and since we cannot carry any great coats on these occasions, we were drenched through before we had gone half a mile.

We went by de Wippe Cabaret Road, and got to the cross roads at six o'clock. Here we had our cookers to meet us, and had our last meal of cold tongue and tea, the men having bread and hot soup. By this time it was pitch dark, not a trace of a moon, and the rain coming down in a solid sheet. We were a very dismal party over dinner, I'm afraid. Took the road at 7.10 again, and had no halt till we got to the High Street, where the Lewis guns had to be picked up. It was very quaint standing in the middle of the main street there in the pitch darkness, and hearing the hoarse voices of the N.C.O.'s and the slush and grind of the hundreds of boots in the muddy road; while every now and again a bursting shell, or the flash from our own guns, would show up the lines of the dripping figures in steel helmets and the shattered remnants of the houses lining the street.

A good many horses lie dead all round the cross roads here, too; and the smell, in view of our business there, was not encouraging.

After a long halt we started off and soon got to the duckboards. From here onwards the walk was a nightmare. There was heavy shelling; the duckboards were broken in many places; and a false step meant at the best going up to your knees in mud, and at the worst up to your neck in a shell hole.

There were frequent long halts in consequence, and on that flat country the rain

drove before the high wind like hailstones,
till one lost all feeling in one's back and
legs. At one time, during a halt, a party
of men coming out of the line met us on
the duckboards and, of course, gave way
to us. As they stood in the mud to their
knees, I heard one man say as we passed
him, " Them as made this bloody war
ought to be made to come out and do it.
We'd —— soon have peace, I know." A
very popular sentiment.

We reached our jumping-off place at
about midnight, still in torrents of rain,
and there proceeded to take up our
stations. We dug trenches and got inside
merely as a protection from shell fire, which
was heavy, and not with any idea of shelter
from the rain; for the trenches themselves
were full of water to the knee before you
had been in five minutes.

Here under a continuous downpour we
remained all night, waiting for Zero, which
was 5.20. The ——s and ——s went over
first and were expected to have an easy

trip; we were to go through them and take Suez Farm, and, still more important, hold it . Very heavy counter-attacks were expected, for the line of Houthoulst Forest being so near our objective, the enemy had an excellent place in which to form up without being seen. I was told to expect heavy casualties and, therefore, as far as possible to leave all cases not desperately wounded, and keep close to the advancing troops, so as to be ready for the casualties at the Farm.

At 5.15 it was just grey in the East. Our guns were keeping up a very heavy fire, and the Boche was plastering us with stuff, too, when suddenly, at 5.20, it seemed as though someone had flung wide the door of hell. I have never heard anything and could never have conceived anything like the volume of sound which our guns made. The sides of my trench shook and rocked, for I put my hand on them to feel; and one's head simply reeled with the roar of the heavies, field guns and " hows.," and the continuous rattle of our machine-gun barrage. Over one's head, rising high amidst the deeper roar, was the ripping, tearing noise of our shells passing across, blended into one long continuous scream. The Boche let loose a tremedous barrage, too, and it was as much as your life was worth to put your head over the top. " They're off," said my Bearer Sergeant to me. I saw his lips move, but although he yelled in my ear I could hear nothing. We lay there another hour waiting for the time for us to go over, and that hour was the worst I have ever spent in my life. We were cold as death ; we were empty (I had breakfasted at Zero off a stick of chocolate and some brandy and water, myself), and it seemed incredible that anything could live under the barrage the Boche had put down for the very purpose of keeping us support troops back.

Well, at 6.30 our bombardment, which had slackened off a bit, again burst out with its old fury ; and, of course, the Boche instantly increased his barrage, since he knew well enough what was to come next. At 6.25 I looked in my surgical haversack to see that I had everything—I had already done so a hundred times !—and then watched the Commanding Officer, who had his watch in his hand.

At 6.40 the men went over the top with a scramble, and at 6.43 the Commanding Officer and Adjutant and I put our heads up and made our little debut. There were a good many men lying on the edge of the trench, and of course these had to be dressed; and so I was left behind almost at once with my bearers. We could make no effort to carry back from there, and so just bound up those we could and hurried after the troops. There was an appalling lot of shelling going on all round, and across the Broembeek there was a barrage like a wall, and it looked really sheer suicide to walk into it.

That was where I envied the troops. They have at least something to kill with and get excited over, while my bearers and I have to walk slowly along about fifty yards behind, doing nothing for long stretches, and able to see everything that goes on. The Boche line was an awful sight, dug-outs blown in, concrete emplacements lying everywhere overturned and dead men all around. Some were half buried; and it was a horrible business to walk past a pair of wildly kicking legs protruding from a ruined dug-out, and know that underneath a man was having the life choked out of him. All the way up we had a fair number of casualties, but not too many, and we reached the Farm at last, which our splendid fellows rushed with the bayonet. Within a minute of schedule time we had taken our final objective and were digging in. Time about ten past eleven.

We made Battalion headquarters in a shell hole, just to the left of the Cemetery at Suez Farm, and I had my aid post in a shell hole along the hedge. The ground

was awfully cut up and muddy, and it was
hopeless to try and make cover for the
wounded, for we were without any mate-
rials. I got the shell hole enlarged a bit
however, and boarded the floor with wood
from a ruined house near by—one bearer
being shot dead by a sniper on his way back
with a load, too—and made slits for myself
and the bearers alongside the hedge. There
were a good many cases in the front line
and the bearers had a devil of a job getting
them in through the mud. The bearers
and I, being the only people moving
around by this time, naturally drew a lot
of fire; and, after a Boche plane had been
over and spotted us they began to shell
our aid post pretty badly, so finally the
C.O. moved his headquarters across the
road into a shell hole about fifty yards
away, and I was left with my bearers at
the aid post. All the afternoon and evening we had a very thin time, and it is a
mystery to me I did not lose more bearers.
I lost six during the first hour clearing

one very nasty bit, and several during the day; but they stuck it magnificently and we had all our front line clear by nightfall.

I had one very near thing myself when I was dressing one of our fellows at the aid post. I was leaning over him, when something went like a broken fiddle string past my ear, and bored a neat hole through the stretcher handle just at my side. I got hold of the fellow by the armpits and just pulled him on top of me into the slit, and they put about three more bullets through the canvas before we got away. We had none of us had any food yet and were really very done up ; but our servants came up about six o'clock and we had hot tea and hard boiled eggs and biscuits, and very good it tasted, too. I had to leave my tea to go to poor —— who was caught by a shell in the line, and died about a minute after I got him in. He was a good fellow. I had walked with him and his Coy. a part of the way up, and it seemed real bad luck to see him come

back all limp, muddy and wet, like a
worried rat, instead of the fine upstanding
fellow he used to be. We had a good
many Boche prisoners wounded and un-
wounded; and as shelling behind us was
too bad for the R.A.M.C. men to clear
cases I used to send my severe ones down
by Boche prisoners in charge of one man,
and got rid of a lot that way. The aid
post was very crowded however, and was
a perfect shambles of mud, rain and blood.
It was quite impossible to get any cover
for anyone. I took the jackets and greatcoats off every prisoner who came through
and used them to cover our men, but they
must have had a hell of a time before
we got them cleared next day. We were
heavily shelled all night; and in the early
morning a flight of Boche planes bombed
us from very low down, and I had several
of my wounded killed that way. I spent
all night either in my slit, sitting in quite
two feet of muddy water, or else dodging
round the aid post trying to explain to

my poor fellows that I had no cover to give them, and had done all that was possible ; but they kept asking to see me every five minutes and one had on the whole a ghastly night. They were wonderfully good though, and kept amazingly quiet, the only noise being from a big Boche N.C.O. who had his leg broken, and he literally howled like a dog and shouted, " Oh, Camerad ! Camerad," till I had him carried out into the middle of the field and planted there. I rather scored off myself in so doing however, for I went round every hour with water for the wounded, and it simply meant I had about fifty yards further to go to him. Finally I had him brought back and he continued to howl till morning. The Boche attacked several times, once at six o'clock and again at dawn, but were crumpled up by our fire both times.

I spent about half an hour talking to one prisoner, a fellow about twenty, who spoke quite good French. I pulled his leg

about the little cakes we had heard they
were selling in Germany, with "Gott straf
England " written on them in icing. He
looked quite ashamed of himself, sitting in
the slit and shuffling his feet about in the
muddy water just like a dirty schoolboy.
I had some Benedictine and brandy in my
water bottle, and while he was holding it
up at me—sort of saying " Good Luck "
before he drank—I chipped in with " Gott
straf England," and he laughed till he
nearly cried.

At about 6.30 a.m. an orderly came running over from Headquarters to say ——
had been wounded. I ran across the road
and found the C.O. and Adjutant crouch-
ing in their shell hole, looking very cold
and battered, and poor old —— lying in
the mud between them. He was lying with
his head hanging back and died as I
opened his shirt. He had been standing
up to stretch himself on the side of the
shell hole after the night's cramping, and
a sniper got him clean through the heart.

I got a bearer across and we carried him back to the aid post, and then I went and had breakfast off cold boiled eggs and tea with the C.O. and Adjutant. We were very depressed all of us, for we had had no food and it was a bitter cold day, and it was a hard job to make dismal jokes and get going again.

We had a hell of a day after that. The Boche counter attacked time after time, and the shelling and machine-gunning was really appalling. Our fellows stuck it magnificently though, which was all the more wonderful since we were everyone of us really done in with the cold and mud. The ambulance men came up about midday and cleared the wounded from a farm about half a mile back; my bearers had to carry to there themselves.

The mud round the aid post had been churned by then into something like seccotine, and it was really a job to get the bearers started, and all of us had to lend a hand to get the four carriers over the

first few yards. Once when we were wrestling with one stretcher, a bearer who was
on the end near me suddenly let go and
pitched forward into the mud, very nearly
bringing us all down. He had been picked
off by a sniper, through the back, and he
died in the aid post about an hour afterwards, poor lad.

About four o'clock we found a small pill
box more or less intact, and as it was
still bitterly cold we moved in there, the
Adjutant, the C.O. and myself; for by this
time we had got all the wounded away
and very few were coming down. The pill
box was a great improvement, for it was
at least warm, but it was here where I had
another very nasty shave. The Adjutant
had sent his servant to look for Boche
greatcoats, and I saw him turning over
several in a heap near the pill box. I
thought one or two might come in useful
if we got any more cases down, so I went
out to him. There were only two, one
clean one and one very muddy one. He

was holding the clean one in his hand, so
I took it off him and moved away back,
and he stooped to pick up the other. Then
I heard an enormous " raang " and a tremendous air concussion nearly threw me
off my feet. I turned round and saw poor
old —— lying about fifteen yards off, all
asprawl. I ran over to him, but he was
stone dead, though there wasn't a mark on
him—killed by the concussion.

The Boche put down a tremendous
amount of stuff between six and eight, for
which we were in a way glad, for it meant
perhaps a quiet night, and as we were to
be relieved by the first Brigade this was
important. We were heavily shelled, however, from our left rear by a big French
gun which was firing short, and for one
hour I honestly thought every minute was
our last. The C.O. sent off messages by
runner, wire and pigeon, but it kept
steadily at it for quite an hour, putting
them literally all around us, till it seemed
incredible we could be missed.

194

At eight o'clock we were relieved and started off down the line; and suddenly all shelling practically ceased, and we had a comparatively peaceful relief. The journey back was awful, for we had a mile and a half more to go than our usual relief, and the ground was up to our waist in places. We finally got to the High Street where we called a halt, and heard that a train would meet us at the Cross Roads at 2 a.m. We slogged down the road, incredibly tired and hungry, and at last we reached our train. They were just ordinary cattle trucks, with bare muddy floors, but we fell into those trucks, officers and men, just as they came, and as we fell on each other so we put our heads down and slept. We were pulled out after a while and marched another two miles to camp, arriving there at 4.15 a.m. The servants who had been left behind had got everyone's kit out and hot baths ready, and Headquarters cooks had got us a really wonderful meal; and to get clean, change

one's absolutely filthy clothes and come
into a warm mess—(for the Quarter-
master had conjured coal from somewhere, and every mess had a stove in it)
—was too exquisite for words. We poured
champagne down in torrents and ate like
nothing on earth, and then staggered off
to bed. I was too tired to take my clothes
off even, and just lay down and slept till
my servant called me next day at 2 p.m.

A quiet day with heavy rain. We heard
in the morning that we were to go as a
Division to the Somne, where it is very
peaceful now, and everyone was very
bucked up. I was very glad, because I did
not really think I could stand any more
shell fire for a while; my head has been
very bad lately and my train of thinking
very disjointed and loose.

Then about five o'clock a message
came to say we were to move into the line

to-morrow night to hold the same bit we had taken. It really is too disgusting, after having just come out after a perfectly monstrous time, to be pitchforked back again. We have had a very quiet dinner, and I shall clear off to bed early. Heard to-day that a shell pitched in the camp of the ——'s to-day, and killed poor ——, their M.O. and got 20 casualties besides. Real bad luck five miles behind the line, and just come out of a push too.

The first news my servant brought with my tea was that the move was cancelled; so that was a load off my mind, and everyone else's. I should have gone on Paris leave to-day, and should certainly have enjoyed it, for I really do feel heady and beastly. I was very glad of it, the idea of sleeping in a real bed at the Ritz and having breakfast in bed under ideal conditions was too enticing. I went across and saw the A.D.M.S. who was awfully decent, but said he really couldn't spare me. We have had three M.O.'s knocked out this last show in the Brigade, and he had no one to do my work. So that's off, confound it. However, I suppose I shouldn't complain; it's better luck than the other poor M.O.'s had anyway.

My servant brought me an enormous apple this morning with my tea—a thing more like a football. He has just come off leave, and said it came off one of the trees in his " old home," and he thought I might like it. I though it awfully nice of him thinking of me, and especially lugging it all the way across in his pack.

We were heavily bombed all round the camp between four o'clock and six this morning, but none fell in the camp actually, thank God. We had some planes over this afternoon observing, so we are pretty sure to get bombed again to-night.

We were heavily bombed last night about seven o'clock, but no casualties. They bombed the ——'s too next door, got nineteen casualties out of them.

At Adjutant's memoranda this morning one N.C.O. giving evidence against a man, on being asked a question, commenced his reply by " Well, sir." The Serjeant Major was on him like a tiger. " What do you mean? I won't have you " welling " in the orderly room! How dare you, don't you know better than that? " The word " welling " fascinated me; it suggested that the unfortunate man had been displaying some strange and unnatural physical phenomenon of a grossly offensive type.

Moved by train to Penton Camp, Proven again. The place is just a large mud heap, and it has rained all day; very dismal.

Nothing doing all day, and very quiet. Some planes came over, and bombed near us last night, but not near enough to worry us.

Got permission to go into Boulogne to-day and had an amusing experience going in. I picked up a motor cyclist and side car, and got a lift for a distance, and then tried to persuade him to take me all the way. He told me that he was having a day off that day, and that if his "boss" who was a "good guy" would let him do it he didn't mind going to Boulogne at all. To his boss we went then; and he disappeared inside to interview him. In a few minutes a very charming old Colonel appeared and said, "I hear you're very anxious to catch the afternoon leave boat." I said, "Yes," thinking that was as good an excuse as any. "Well, under the circumstances, I'll be very glad to let my driver take you in," said he; "will you come in and have some breakfast before you start?" I thanked him and went into the mess, where about six other men were. We were a very cheery party; I had got a day off and wonderful prospects, and was at the very acme of my form, and breakfast went like a wedding bell. Once or twice I thought I caught a curious intent look in the Colonel's eye, but put it down to a habit.

When I left he came to see me off, and said "Well, goodbye and good luck. I hope you'll not find things as bad as you think on the other side." "Thanks very much," said I, and tried to put some feeling into my voice, though what he meant was a mystery.

When we had gone a little distance at an average interval of a hairbreadth from eternity—my driver liking, as he phrased it, " to feel her travel some "—" What was it you told your C.O." I asked. "Oh! I just said you'd heard your mother was dying, and wanted to get home quick," was the reply.

Years hence, when the talk in the

smoke-room veers round to murderers and
their callous feelings, I can hear that dear
old Colonel say " Talking of callousness,
I remember a doctor fellow coming into
our mess once "—and then out will come
my whole horrid story!

Moved this morning to Houlle, near
St. Omer, leaving Camp at 3 a.m. It was
drizzling rain, and had been raining
heavily all night, and as my tent lets it
through all over, the Adjutant and I had
a rotten time.

Got to Houlle about midday, and find
very comfortable billets. We are to be
here I believe about three weeks and then
go to the Somme again.

I am billeted with our transport officer,
a perfectly delightful soul, but who constantly makes one doubt the wisdom of
our English educational system. When we
went into our room, there was a large
picture over the fireplace—" Le Retour de

Calvaire." Before this he halted, and gazed critically at the stream of mourners on their woe-begone little mules and donkeys winding disconsolately down the hill. He is a passionate lover of animals, and looked a picture of melodrama in his breeches, boots and spurs, the keen eyes peering out of his lean tanned face.

Finally he turned to me. " Look at this, Doc, 'The return of the Cavalry.' But did you ever see such a collection of horses? " I agreed with him, but it was an exquisite moment!

Had a splendid night, a real bed and a roof over me; slept like a log.

Have had very bad pains and sickness this last week, I guess I have caught a chill.

Had a quiet night, some bombing over St. Omer, but none near us, although planes came over about 4 a.m. Had a charming ride this morning out to the range with the Colonel and Adjutant; a glorious crisp September morning with diaphanous wisps of mist in the hollows. The country here is exactly like that round Beachy Head. The clumps of trees are already a lovely brown, with here and there splashes of white where a chalk quarry lies, or a snow white church peers up to mark a village. I was rather disappointed to find I stand noise so badly yet. I had to leave the range while the rapid firing was on.

The Duke of Connaught reviewed us at one o'clock. The Battalion looked very smart drawn up on the crest of the hill with the long straight poplar-lined road stretching away behind it towards Calais, and the village children standing on the low wall by the Cabaret.

A charming day. Went into St. Omer and had tea. Coming out by an ambulance we heard the Boche killed 57 of his own wounded in the hospital there last night, so that's all to the good. I saw a nurse I knew and talked awhile with her, and incidentally told her I was trying to get a bath in St. Omer and found them all full up. She suggested I could have one in their hospital baths if I cared to come out, so away I went. Got there to find a perfectly wonderful installation, porcelain baths and any amount of hot water. Had a perfectly gorgeous bath; and on going into the massage room next door to dry myself as I had been told, found my friend mending my clothes for me. On the whole, what with gratitude for the bath, and that exquisite languor induced by it, I fear I took longer drying myself than I have hitherto found necessary.

205

Another quiet night, but found it raining hard when I woke this morning. Had a very dirty walk round the billets, and then spent the rest of the afternoon on my bed reading. It is a treat to have nothing to do for a while, and to have peace and quiet also to do it in.

I should have gone to Paris to-day, but one of our officers has just heard his father is in Paris, so I let him go instead. I shall be very glad to get there myself, however.

Walked round the transport in the morning and in the afternoon had a delightful ride with the Second in Command through the forest. The colours of the trees were simply wonderful, all gold, orange and red; and in the thin October sun the whole forest looked like a theatrical scene. Came back with a tremendous appetite for dinner, read " Sex and Character " for a while, smoked a cigar, and so to bed.

To-morrow we leave for the Somme, where we hear things are very quiet. I look forward to the next few weeks immensely. Life with a Battalion is at all times fascinating; but when one is to be out of the line for some time it approaches more nearly to the joys of the " reading parties " of happy memory than anything I have ever experienced. One has a definite job to do—well within one's powers, too. One is out of doors continually; and life is simplified to such an extent that the commonest details acquire a new savour. One dips idly into books, and finds therein an unaccustomed charm; one debates after dinner with portentous solemnity or airy badinage; and one's cigar partakes almost of the nature of a sacrament. In such an atmosphere of youth as permeates the mess, one recaptures, in fact, some shadow of those halcyon days when Life was but a gay adventure, and " troubles " just a synonym for " spice."

PART V

Courcelle le Comte.

We reached here last night after an uneventful journey down South. We heard last night from the C.O. that instead of, as we had been told, going down to take over from the French at St. Quentin, we were designed to take part in a gigantic push against Douai and Cambrai with the idea of breaking through the Boche line. The whole thing has been most carefully camouflaged, even to the extent of having it given out in the French Chamber that we were to take over line from them. Moreover, everyone in the Division has been kept in darkness as to the real intention, so that it is hoped to take the Boche completely by surprise.

At 6.15 there was a great deal of gun-

ning on our front, so the attack has
evidently been launched, but up to now
(2.30 p.m.) we have heard no news of its
progress. It is raining hard, too, which
will of course hinder the advance enormously. It is very wearing sitting here
waiting for orders; everyone is keyed up
to a tremendous pitch; we have cut down
our kit to an irreducible minimum which
has to be carried by each man personally,
and life is at present a pretty ghastly one.
This camp is not a bad one really—Nissen
huts, no fires, and plenty of mud—but the
cold and rain are a devil. Our job in this
push is to take the final objectives, and
hold them against the counter attacks the
Boche will make with fresh troops dashed
down here by train; so again we look like
having a stiff job.

4.30 p.m.

A wire has just come from Division to
say that so far everything has been very
successful. We had just started tea when
the orderly brought the wire in, and the

excitement was intense. An officer was sent to tell the Coys. and the bursts of cheering from the various huts were quite good to hear.

Last night was the coldest I have spent for some time. All our kit was packed; and the stuff we carried so cut down for transport purposes that we just lay down in our clothes, pulled our overcoats over us, and lay awake like that. It rained in torrents almost all night, and blew a gale, and the draughts in the huts were appalling. As we had no fire in the mess we cleared off early " to bed," since the mess was like an ice house; and having no seats of any sort either, it was not too tempting to stay in.

News continues to be good, though Flesquieres has held our troops up for some hours.

Raining all day and the camp a sea of mud. I have given a first-aid lecture and otherwise done nothing all day, waiting for orders to move. I hope it has cleared up by then; a march in this rain and then a night in the same clothes would not be too attractive.

We left camp at 7 p.m. in a steady drizzle, 'buses being supposed to meet us at 8 p.m. at some cross roads about three miles away. As I stood by the quarter-master's stores, where all kits had been dumped, it was very interesting to hear the comments of the men as they filed past to get on the road. There was a broad beam of light coming from the stores, and the men inside gave it a curiously English-railway-station look. This caught the fancy of many of the men as they passed. " All French money changed here " one man said; and another " I've missed my last train home I know," and so on, every-one being in high spirits. The road was

quite eighteen inches deep in soft slush,
and the march to the cross roads was not
too delightful. There was no moon and
no wind; just a heavy steamy mist of rain
which made one sweat under one's pack
and coat. We arrived at the 'bus rendez-
vous at 8 p.m., and remained standing in
an incredibly muddy field by the roadside,
waiting for our 'buses. There was a good
deal of gunning going on, and the flashes
looked most picturesque behind the mist.
One hour passed, and two hours, and still
no 'buses; and one began to get very cold
and dismal, since our last meal had been
at 4.30. The men sang songs and were
generally the wonderful people they always
are under such conditions, but the mud
was awfully cold to one's feet, and one's
clothes soughed on one's back as one
moved. At 1.45, almost six hours after
we had arrived there, a bright glow began
to appear in the sky over the rise in the
Arras-Bapaume Road; and shortly one
was treated to a really lovely sight.

The road ran at an angle to meet ours, and in a very few minutes some 300 'buses were defiling at regular distances along it. Their headlights, so evenly spaced along the broad sweep of the road, the intervening tract of shiny sodden earth, and the whole lit by a misty moon just newly risen, looked exactly like the lights along the Thames Embankment as seen from the Surrey shore. The men raised a hearty cheer as they drew alongside us, and clambered in like schoolboys going to a picnic. After a very wet ride along a crowded road, we passed through Bapaume and reached our camp at last—time 7.10—just over twelve hours to do eight miles! We had hot soup and some stewed steak, and fell into our blankets as we were and slept till 12.30 to-day.

The Brigadier came into our hut before we were up this morning, said the attack was going very well, and that we should ourselves move again to-morrow morning. Went for a short walk through Le Trans-

213

loy and came back to tea. Eighteen
hundred prisoners passed our camp just
before tea, some of them very fine fellows,
obviously new troops rushed down to meet
the attack.

La Buquiere.

Reached here last night.

A very dreary march, bitterly cold and
a steady rain falling, the roads being incredibly muddy and rough. We hear now
that the tanks were held up ultimately,
and that the big break through was
stopped, so I suppose our job will come
pretty soon now. As we were marching
through one village we saw a caterpillar
drawing guns up, which was being kept
back by the limber and horses of a field
gun which had been caught by a shell,
just before we got there. The whole thing
was a hopeless tangle of dead men and
horses and the remains of the gun and
limber, and the cross roads were a mass

of standing troops waiting to get past. As time was very valuable and there were no tools near to lift the limber, the caterpillar just backed a bit and drove over everything, dead horses limber and all, flattening a road for itself and us like a crimson carpet at a nightmare wedding. I've seldom seen a more unpleasant sight. Arrived in camp about midnight and found just a few tents in a big mud-field; everything saturated with water. We had no place for a mess, and just hung a wagon sheet over poles and dined under that. There were no fires, and the wind blowing through our wet clothes was simply awful. There is heavy drum fire on our front to-night, evidently an attack going on. Word has just come from Brigade that we are at ten-minutes' notice to hold the front line. It certainly can't be any more unpleasant than this.

215

Just before going to bed we heard we had attacked and failed to take Bourlon Wood, and that the ——th Division were to attack again at dawn. If they failed we were to be put over. We were heavily shelled by a big naval gun all night, and at 4.15 were ordered to march. We naturally thought we should be for the Wood, but at ten we heard the ——th had taken most of it and the village, so we were to move further on. It was very pretty in camp at dawn, or rather just before. The tents were all covered with hoar-frost and gleamed so fresh and clear in the cold light. There was a thick ground mist on too, and only the tent tops showed above it, like mountain peaks over the clouds. The cold was simply awful however; one was almost too cold to eat. We had an interesting march, though the long-range shelling in places was very nasty, and we had a few casualties. The country was literally covered with troops—cavalry, infantry and artillery everywhere. We

reached the Hindenburg line about midday, and were halted here in a ravine. We
were very hungry by this time, and it was
very cold, too, standing about; so we
lunched off cold bully beef and whiskey
and water which was all we had, and
indeed all we are likely to have for some
days now, for all our hot stuff has been
left behind to save transport. I had a very
interesting time afterwards wandering
about over the old Boche line, and looking
at the derelict tanks which are everywhere.
The wire here is simply incredible, 50
yards deep and as thick as a wall; no
infantry could have possibly got through
it unaided. The tanks seem to have had
a very easy time however; there are very
few dead about, and not many shell holes.
The proof that we took him by surprise
however, is everywhere to be seen. One
Boche in the trench was evidently mending a pair of woollen gloves when he was
killed, for the needle still lay in the glove
by him when I found him. A good many

of them still lie on the steps of the dug-out, too, just where they had fallen while running out, still with their boots off. There are a good many of them in the dug-outs where they were bombed, and it is very unpleasant getting them up the stairs. The dug-outs themselves are amazing, though; quite fifty feet deep and boarded throughout, with nine beds and two entrances each. Headquarters is in a machine-gun headquarters of theirs, which has a periscope so that they could look out over no-man's land with safety. We have got fires here to-night, for there is plenty of wood about, and it is a Godsend to get warm again, though we are all very dirty, having slept in our clothes now for several days. There is a derelict tank just higher up the trench here, which got stuck on its end going over. It looks exactly like some pre-historic beast looking out over the country-side in the dusk. There is a good deal of shelling all round here; the Boche is just on the hill crest opposite us, and we are under direct observation except when in the trench. We shall probably be bombed to-night.

Had a very tedious night. The beds here are just hard planks, and the air is very stuffy down below, too. The rats are unique. They are everywhere, and run over your bed and leap on the floor like cats or rabbits. There was an awful noise of shelling, too, and although nothing could reach us down there, the air concussion bothered my head a good deal.

Went with the C.O. to make his reconnaissance in the afternoon, and had a very interesting time. We climbed on to the hill the other side of Flesquieres and could see Amieux, Bourlon, Fontaine, and Cambrai as clear as though we were ten yards off instead of a mile or more. While we were there the Boche counter-attacked Bourlon, and it was a wonderful sight to

see the battle like that going on before
one's very eyes. It's the first bit of real
open fighting I have ever seen and was
simply thrilling. We had a rather bad time
going over the open to find a road for the
Battalion to-night, for the Boche was
shelling Orival Wood very heavily, and
several came very unpleasantly near,
covering us with dirt several times. We
sheltered for half an hour in a dug-out on
the road, during an amazing snow-storm
which came on like magic and lasted only
a short time. Coming home we saw the
tanks which had been knocked out by one
Boche gun outside Flesquieres, and some
of them were very badly knocked about.
One of them had had a direct hit, and the
shell had exploded the shells inside her,
too; and the tank's interior was just a
butcher's scrap-heap smeared over everything, all eight of the crew being just
blown to ribbons. We got back about six
o'clock after a very interesting day. Saw
a pitfall for a tank, camouflaged to look

like a trench—very cleverly done. Had a talk to a fellow salving tanks, too, and he gave me a ride in one. It's really uncanny to feel yourself go over a trench or through a hedge. It will spoil me for traffic at home, if I ever get back again!

Got up this morning at five to dress some of our fellows who had been caught by a shell while souvenir-hunting in the open! It was very unpleasant, cold, raining and a good deal of shelling, too. Spent a very quiet day looking round.

We go into the line at six to-night; it's bitterly cold and raining hard, so we look like having a poor tour. The men are very fit and keen, however; there isn't a sick man among them, so we should stand it well enough.

Later.

In billets at Ruyalcourt.

This last three days has been the most

heartbreaking time I have ever known in my life. We left the Hindenburg line at 6 p.m. on the 26th, to hold the Bourlon line. It was an awful night, an icy wind and fine sleet falling, and we got to La Justice Farm about eight o'clock. Here we were suddenly halted, made to take up artillery formation in the field on the left of the road and kept there for four solid hours. The cold was literally awful; and as we had had our last meal at four o'clock, we were pretty hungry, too. At last the C.O. came back, called up all the Coy. Commanders and me and told us we had to attack Fontaine Notre Dame at dawn. As we had heard a few days before that this was hopeless to attempt, we were all pretty cheered up at the news. However, no one said anything, and as we were going back to the Battalion the C.O. said to me that I was to use my own discretion about leaving or bringing the wounded out. "We are to expect no artillery support, and no support troops," he said, " so we'll just

222

have to do our damnedest on our own."
We went up to the line and I made my aid
post in Containg Mill. It snowed and
blew all night and was intensely cold and
the Boche shelled us heavily all the time.
We went over at 6.20 led by two tanks.
I have never known such machine-gun fire
as we met going across the first hundred
yards. They just sounded like a continuous scream. The Boche put down a terrific barrage, too, and our poor lads went
down like grass before a reaper. They
still kept steadily on though, and we
reached the village on time. I got a good
many walking wounded back, but the fire
was hopeless for bearers, and I had half of
them knocked out before the village was
reached, so I had to keep the rest near me
to help dress cases. The village was literally hell. There were Boche everywhere,
but we got a good many prisoners however, and I sent back a lot of stretcher
cases by them. One fellow didn't want to
carry and I had to clout him over the

head to make him lend a hand. When we
got back to the aid post he sat down on
the steps of the dug-out, and every time I
came near him he kept plucking me by
the coat and saying something. I took no
notice of him, but it struck me as curious
that he hadn't gone downstairs to be
gorged with "enemy" cocoa and bread, as
most of them do at once. Finally a shell
pitched quite near us, and blew the roof
off the shelter I'd made over the dug-out
entrance. It put the wind up me all right,
but when I turned round there he was still
sitting quietly as before, and I knew he
must be hit or something. I went over to
him, and when I saw his face I was certain.
He didn't look hurt, he looked dead, and
dead a long time at that. Then I saw he
was holding his trousers together with one
hand; and when I pulled his hand away
the entire contents of his belly just spilled
itself over his knees. I tucked them in
again, covered him up, and gave him two
grains of morphia to suck. It was the best

I could do for him, poor devil. But I wish
now I hadn't hit him. I wish that quite a
lot. On my way back I saw another Boche
with both legs blown off pulling himself
along the road on his chest and elbows—
a perfectly ghastly sight. Poor —— was
killed just outside the church; a machine-
gun bullet got him clean through the throat
and he died immediately. No. 4 Coy.
reached its final objective with 15 men and
one N.C.O. only.

We held our final objective for about an
hour, though the fighting was terrific; but
when the Boche counter-attacked with
fresh troops we just hadn't enough men
left and had to fight our way out again.
We ended up finally in our jumping-off
trenches that we had left in the morning.
We went in 680 and 19 officers, and we
came out 135 and 6 officers, and we should
have been wiped out completely without
any doubt if the men had not remained so
steady as they did, for they just fought
every inch of the way back and never gave

ground until ordered to. We held the line until nightfall and were then relieved, and marched to the cross roads near La Justice. I could have cried to see the Battalion coming out. They had gone in such a splendid lot of fellows, and they made such a pitiful show as they came out, marching in a solid body it's true, though some companies were only fifteen or twenty men, and responding always to the " Get hold of it," of the N.C.O.'s, but looking so done and dismal as I've never seen them before. There was no singing and very little talking, for every man of us knew we had failed, and one felt that every one we passed knew it, too. I have never been more wretched, tired and hungry and dispirited, and at the same time feeling we had been let down somehow by somebody.

We spent the night in dug-outs fearfully crowded, so that many of the men slept on the stairs.

The next day we marched here and got in about eight o'clock. We are to go out and rest and refit for a month they say, and not before we need it. I hope to get on leave now. The Brigadier came in after lunch and told us that the Boche was preparing a tremendous attack on our line opposite Fontaine, and that we were put in to break it and hold him till more troops could be brought down. He tells us that the Battalion was never expected to do as much as it did, and certainly no one imagined we should even take the village, let alone hold it. He brought a very charming message from the Divisional General, saying we had saved the situation, but after all that's not much consolation for losing almost the entire Battalion.

Later.

We heard on the morning of the 30th that the Boche had broken through at Gonnelieu, taken Gonnelieu and Gouzeaucourt, and was somewhere in the open pushing all before him. We received orders to join our Brigade and make a counter-attack.

We joined the Brigade about 3 p.m. and came on the Boche marching down the main road, just outside Gouzeaucourt. We pushed him back and retook the village, losing fairly heavily.

We spent the night in the open, just in front of the village. The cold was awful; there was some snow and we were shelled and bombed all night. In the morning the news was much better, as our Division seems to have the Boche well in hand, and has pushed him almost all the way back and is holding the line all right.

Battalion Headquarters is in dug-outs in a sunken road, very badly knocked about by shell fire. The Boche has it taped off, too, and every now and then will put a salvo of eight all round the door, which makes my visits to my aid post higher up very unpleasant indeed.

The first evening we were in we heard that a prisoner, captured the day before, had said that a very heavy attack was to be made on our front early the next morning; and of course we expected trouble. We really should be cleaned up altogether if he came on in real force, for we are holding a lot of line, and all of us are very done up. The troops on our right are native cavalry and some of the Division which bolted the first day, so we can expect no support from them. They have sent up a Battalion of ——s to counter-attack if we are wiped out, so the line ought to hold anyway. We have orders to hold the line at all costs. The Boche attacked at dawn, the first day, and we beat him off. Fortunately we took about 40 machine-guns out of Gouzeaucourt, so we can get some stuff over, and our men will stand till the last. He must have lost very heavily. He attacked several times last night, too, and again this morning, but was beaten off each time, and fortunately he has never come against us in too big numbers. The shelling is very bad, however, and we are getting casualties all the time. He put a shell right into our Headquarters' door this morning, and nearly buried us all under about a ton of earth. We got out at the other door all right though. Very unpleasant, however.

Our water supply is getting very low too, the barrage is too bad for transport to get up, and we shall be very glad when some other Division can be found to hold this line. There was a very heavy attack on the next village to us this morning, but the 3rd Brigade must have beaten it off. We have had a good many casualties to-day. I have a perfectly monstrous head to-night.

Another scare at dawn; tremendous shelling and many casualties. Attack beaten off, however. It's bitterly cold to-

day and some snow is falling. The 1st
——s came up to-day; they are to relieve
us to-night. They look a very good lot,
and should hold on all right, for they are
up to full strength. They came at tea-
time, and the Boche blew the candles out
about ten times in the hour with 5.9's.
They didn't seem too cheered up at the
prospect.

We left Irvine Lane at 6 p.m. and had
rather a bad relief, being heavily shelled
all the way out. Came back to Gouzeaucourt Wood to find tents up. We have no
kit, however, and it was bitterly cold sleeping on the ground in one's overcoat. We
were heavily bombed at dawn, too; and
that and a 12-inch howitzer firing every
hour just behind us has just about done
my head in completely. The Boche attacked again at dawn but must have been

231

beaten off all right by the 1st ——s, but it put the wind up us all. We now expect every orderly who comes from the Brigade to be bringing a message to say we have to hold the line again. We'll all be very glad to get out of this area. We are supposed to go out to-night, and as I write this there is a tremendous barrage coming down on our front, so we may still not get away.

The main feature in life at present for me is that I go on leave as soon as we get out of this area. That prospect fills my entire horizon to the exclusion of everything else.

Later. Royalcourt.

Got back here in billets by train, and I start on leave this evening.

Envoi.

On my return to England certain symptoms developed which necessitated my return to hospital, and shortly before the Armistice I was invalided from the Army altogether. So ended an unforgettable experience; and it is curious, in retrospect, to find how much one had enjoyed it. One had shared a common task with men of every type and station, and had been admitted therefore to a fellowship and intimacy so rare as to outweigh even the beastliness which made it possible. The tragedy of the war is not that so many lives were lost and so many ideals shattered, but that this intimacy and fellowship —bought with so much agony and tears— should have been lost to the world in the end. Had there been, at the time of peace, one man in the world so big as to have kept this fellowship undimmed, never since Christ was crucified would a sacrifice have been so worth while. But the one man was lacking, and we are all where we

233

were before—speaking a strange tongue one to another, and suspecting and guarding against an animosity which does not exist. We are no longer sharing a common burden, but bitterly competing one with another for a purse for our own advancement; and an enmity formerly reserved for Germans must therefore now include the man next door. And that I suppose is the truth of it—that only in mutual service lies the real hope of mankind.